Your Towns and Cities in

Plymouth
in the Great War

Your Towns and Cities in the Great War

Plymouth
in the Great War

Derek Tait

Pen & Sword
MILITARY

First published in Great Britain in 2014 by
PEN & SWORD MILITARY
an imprint of
Pen and Sword Books Ltd
47 Church Street
Barnsley
South Yorkshire S70 2AS

Copyright © Derek Tait, 2014

ISBN 978 1 78346 285 8

A CIP record for this book is available from the British Library

Printed and bound in England
by CPI Group (UK) Ltd, Croydon, CR0 4YY

Typeset in Times New Roman by Chic Graphics

Pen & Sword Books Ltd incorporates the imprints of
Pen & Sword Archaeology, Atlas, Aviation, Battleground, Discovery,
Family History, History, Maritime, Military, Naval, Politics, Railways,
Select, Social History, Transport, True Crime, and Claymore Press,
Frontline Books, Leo Cooper, Praetorian Press, Remember When,
Seaforth Publishing and Wharncliffe.

For a complete list of Pen and Sword titles please contact
Pen and Sword Books Limited
47 Church Street, Barnsley, South Yorkshire, S70 2AS, England
E-mail: enquiries@pen-and-sword.co.uk
Website: www.pen-and-sword.co.uk

Contents

Acknowledgements

Thanks to John Van Der Kiste, Steve Johnson, Daisy Parker, Derek Parker, Benjamin Pile, Alan Tait, Ellen Tait, Bruce E Hunt, Tina Cole and Tilly Barker.

CHAPTER 1

1914

Eager for a Fight

Plymouth at the beginning of 1914 was a prosperous town, one of the three towns that would later make up the city in 1928. The two other nearby towns were Devonport and Stonehouse. Amalgamation of the towns took place on 1 November 1914.

Rising tensions in Europe and the assassination of Franz Ferdinand in Sarajevo led to Austria-Hungary's declaration of war on Serbia. This led to the Central Powers, which included Germany and Austria-Hungary, and the Allies, which included the British Empire, the French Republic and the Russian Empire, to declare war on each other, which led to the commencement of the First World War on 28 July 1914.

Archduke Franz Ferdinand of Austria. Ferdinand's assassination in Sarajevo on 28 June 1914 led to Austria-Hungary's declaration of war on Serbia, which ultimately led to the beginning of the First World War.

In the early hours of 3 August, the Cunard Canadian service liner *Andania* entered Plymouth Sound in darkness. A British torpedo boat destroyer came alongside. An officer on the destroyer questioned the liner's captain through a megaphone and requested that he dismantle his wireless equipment before proceeding. It was noted that all wireless stations not required by the government were being taken down.

On 3rd August, it was reported in the *Eugene Register* that:

Passengers arriving today from Montreal on the Cunard line steamer Andania, *bound for South Empson, reported that the vessel was met at sea by a British torpedo boat and ordered by wireless to stop. The liner then was led into Plymouth as a matter of precaution against mines. Plymouth was found filled with soldiers and searchlights were seen constantly flashing about the harbour.*

On 3 August, there was much excitement when it was announced that the German liner *Kronprinzessen Cecilie*, travelling from New York to Bremmen, carrying £2,000,000 in gold in her strongroom, would be landing at Plymouth. Also on board were 1,600 mailbags and 150 passengers. However, she abandoned her call at Plymouth and it was reported that she had been sighted off Malin Head on the North coast of Ireland. Speculation in the newspapers suggested that her commander, Captain C. Polack, would try to get to his destination via the north of Scotland. However, the ship later returned to the United States to avoid capture by the British Navy and French cruisers.

On 4 August, just before midnight, the offices of the *Western Morning News* in Plymouth posted an announcement in their window that Britain had declared war on Germany. One of the newspaper journalists recorded:

SS Kronprinzessin Cecilie. *On 3 August 1914, there was much excitement when it was announced that the SS* Kronprinzessin Cecilie, *carrying £2,000,000 in gold, would be landing at Plymouth. However, the call at port was abandoned and the ship later returned to the United States to avoid capture by the British Navy and French cruisers.*

The news caused a profound sensation, several women swooning,
and a long murmur of excitement passed through the crowd.

Many people were asleep in their beds and knew nothing of the
announcement until the following day when official war notices were
placed in newspaper publishers' windows and on placards. Newspapers
were soon full of the news.

On the day that war was declared residents living in Devonport
recalled being kept awake all night as mules and carts carried guns and
ammunition out of the dockyard.

People of foreign descent were quickly rounded up and detained.
Anyone with a German-sounding accent soon came under suspicion
of being a spy. On the evening of 4 August, three men were arrested as
they tried to make their way through recently constructed wire
entanglements beside Plymouth Sound.

Soon after the announcement, people began panic buying which
drove prices up and caused a shortage. The mayor appealed for
restraint.

The declaration of hostilities was seen by many with excitement.
The war meant more activity in the dockyard, which would lead to

Gladys Cuddeford and her horse, which was later requisitioned for the war. Horses
fared badly at the Front and were not expected to return. For many it was a
heartbreaking experience being parted from their animals. The Cuddefords were tenant
farmers at Barne Farm between 1883 and 1916.

more employment with more ships needing to be built and serviced. Men employed at the dockyard found that their wages increased and were offered overtime and wartime bonuses.

Many felt that the war would all be over by Christmas and there was great enthusiasm as well as patriotism.

The railways were taken under government control under the Regulations of Forces Act of 1871. Local businesses were asked to supply motor vehicles for use by the army and the many farms in and around Plymouth were asked to supply horses.

One horse taken away belonged to Gladys Cuddeford of Barne Farm.

Horses fared badly at the front. Many were killed by artillery fire and were affected by skin conditions and poison gas. Hundreds of thousands of horses died during the conflict. Many horses were requisitioned from British civilians. However, Lord Kitchener stated that no horse under 15 hands should be confiscated. This was because

Two soldiers take care of one of their horses. Casualties amongst horses in the artillery and transport divisions were high but soldiers of the Army Veterinary Corps worked hard to relieve any suffering. All wounds and injuries were carefully treated. Here a sergeant sews up a wound on a horse's nose.

many children showed a concern about the welfare of their ponies.

Central government delegated the provision of shells to local committees. The headquarters for the south-west were in Bristol, and Plymouth's own munitions committee formed part of that.

Contracts were issued from Bristol for the supply of shells but only from companies that were able to supply at least 100 shells a week. No company in Plymouth could meet this quota so a combination was

A female shell worker. During the war 900,000 women were employed in munition factories. Volunteers came from all social classes and the work was said to be hard as well as dangerous.

worked out, with Plymouth becoming a sub-contractor to a Mr Priest. The shells were made in Plymouth and then the explosives, charging and fusing were added in Bristol. Plymouth was paid 11s 3d for each shell case. The shells were made at the Plymouth and Devonport Technical Schools under the supervision of a Mr Govier, who was the metalwork teacher. This was agreed to by Mr Burns Brown, the principal.

A drilling machine and lathe were brought in from the electricity works at Prince Rock and two other lathes were borrowed from the tramway department.

Large numbers of women underwent training so that they could manufacture the shell cases. The higher education sub-committee of Plymouth Council made sure that all the women were interviewed before they were employed.

Many schools were converted into hospitals in preparation for the return of wounded soldiers from the Front. The Devonport Higher Elementary School was converted in 1914 and the Devonport Technical School also became a temporary hospital in the same year.

On Wednesday 5 August, Salisbury Road School was requisitioned and the Territorial Army moved in to remove desks and other fixings. On Friday 7 August, Messrs Spooner's Ltd arrived with all the ordnance supplies, equipment and signs needed.

The Territorial Force of the Devonshire Regiment included the 1/5th (Prince of Wales') Battalion formed in Millbay in August. They were part of the Devon & Cornwall Brigade, Wessex Division.

A report in the *Evening Herald* of 6 August read:

The authorities have taken over control of the two railways serving the town. The military authorities earlier informed Plymouth firms owning horses that they would have to provide the Army with a number of animals. People watched with keen interest the parade of horses in the streets and the inspection by the officers making the selection. Motor wagons belonging to various local firms were also borrowed. At the request of Major-General A. P. Penton, the Fortress Commander, a representative of each of the Three Towns attended at the offices of the South-West Coast Defences. Major-General Penton said that it was his intention during the present crisis to deal with only one authority for the whole of the Three Towns.

The three representatives agreed that the Mayor of Plymouth should be the representative with whom the major-general shall deal. Excitement was heightened during the day by some unfounded rumours. Weeping women were to be seen in all parts of the towns.

On 6 August, the *North Devon Journal* reported that the 6th Devons, who had been camped at Woodbury, were to be moved to Plymouth after a despatch order had been received. The order called for their immediate removal to Barnstable but was changed and they were told to make their way to Plymouth. Special trains carried them from Exeter to Plymouth where they proceeded to the Drill Hall at Millbay, where arrangements had been made to billet the men.

Also, on 6 August, *HMS Amphion*, a Devonport-based cruiser, became the first Royal Navy casualty of the war.

On the previous day *Amphion* and the 3rd Flotilla received a report from a trawler that a ship had been spotted 'throwing things overboard'. The trawler gave the ship's position and *Amphion* and the flotilla set off to investigate. Soon after they spotted the German minelayer *SMS Königin Luise* heading eastwards.

HMS Amphion *was the first Royal Naval ship to be sunk during the First World War. On 6 August, she struck a mine that had been laid by the German minelayer SMS Königin Luise. Further mines were hit and the ensuing explosion destroyed the ship. Approximately 150 British sailors were killed.*

Königin Luise was a requisitioned former Hamburg-Netherlands holiday ferry that had been converted into an auxiliary minelayer.

On the evening of 4 August, she had left Emden on a course for the North Sea with the intent of laying mines off the Thames Estuary. *Königin Luise* was disguised in the colours of steamers of the Great Eastern Railway, which were black, buff and yellow. The genuine steamers travelled from Harwich to the Hook of Holland.

Königin Luise's attempt to escape aroused suspicion from the approaching fleet and four destroyers, including *Landrail* and *Lance*, gave chase. Within the hour *Königin Luise* was sunk by its pursuers. From a crew of 100 there were forty-six survivors and *Amphion* picked up many of these before continuing on its pre-arranged search of the waters.

The destroyers soon located another ship of the same shape and colour as the *Königin Luise,* this time flying a large German flag. The destroyers opened fire. However, *Amphion* realised that the ship was in fact the *St Petersburg*. On board was the German Ambassador returning to Germany from England. *Amphion* signalled to the destroyers to cease fire but they continued. *Amphion* positioned itself between the destroyers and the *St Petersburg*, which allowed the ship to continue on its journey safely.

They continued to search the waters until 03.30 am on 6 August when they returned to Harwich. However, their course ran close to where *Königin Luise* had placed mines and at 06.30 am, *Amphion*

The SMS Königin Luise *was a German-requisitioned former Hamburg-Netherlands holiday ferry that had been converted into an auxiliary minelayer and was ultimately responsible for the sinking of HMS* Amphion *on 6 August 1914.*

struck one, killing many men on board while also incapacitating the captain. When the captain recovered he ran to the engine room to shut down the engines. The vessel's back was already broken and the escorting destroyers returned to rescue *Amphion's* crew. At the same time they rescued several German survivors. Although the engines had been shut down, *Amphion* continued to drift towards the minefield and at 07.30 am struck a row of mines, which shot debris over the rescue boats and destroyers. A shell from *Amphion* hit the deck of *Lark* killing two of *Amphion's* rescued crew as well as a German prisoner. *Amphion* sank within fifteen minutes of the last explosion. Almost 150 British sailors were killed as well as eighteen of the crew rescued from *Königin Luise*.

Kitchener's recruitment poster, Your country needs you! *A huge recruitment campaign encouraged young men to join up. By January 1915, almost one million men had enlisted. Pals battalions encouraged many to enlist and they ultimately provided enough men for three battalions.*

At home, Plymouth Argyle had been making plans to join the Football League when war intervened. Professional football continued to be played up and down the country, although there were some objections while men were fighting and being killed overseas. Lord Kitchener's campaign, which included posters stating 'Your country needs you', appealed for fit young men to join the army. Many footballers from all over Britain answered the call, including several players from Plymouth Argyle. Criticism of football was voiced locally because of the three towns' strong military tradition. Local newspapers stopped reporting on match results so they could include page after page of those wounded or killed in battle.

In the summer of 1914, Moses Russell joined Plymouth Argyle. He received a record fee of £400.

On 7 August, *Vindictive*, a British light cruiser, captured the German steamer *Schlesien* and took her into the port at Plymouth. The 3,328-ton steamer was en route from Brisbane to Bremen when she was captured.

On 8 August, the 3rd (Reserve) Battalion of the Devonshire Regiment moved from Exeter to Plymouth.

HMS Vindictive. *On 7 August 1914,* Vindictive *captured the German steamer* Schlesien *and took her into the port at Plymouth. On 21 November, an auction was held in Plymouth selling off goods recovered from the ship and other naval prizes including 328 bags of white pepper, sixty-five bags of rice, fifty-five bags of cinnamon bark, 100 cases of sticklac and forty-five bales of hemp tow.*

On 11 August, a matron, sixty-eight staff nurses and twenty-two sisters began work at the newly converted Salisbury Road Hospital. Also located within the building were a treatment centre and a neurological section as well as 280 beds. The hospital opened on 17 August.

An announcement in the *Exeter and Plymouth Gazette* stated that Mount Edgcumbe Park would not be open for the forseeable future due to the war. A bazaar that was to be held there to help reduce the debt of the Bideford Church Institute was postponed indefinitely.

On 12 August, the Austrian steamer, *Mediterranes*, loaded with a cargo of barley, arrived in Plymouth in the charge of a naval crew.

On Tuesday 18 August, newspapers reported that there had been such a rapid rate of men enlisting in England that the recruiting service was almost paralysed. Approximately 7,000 men had joined up in

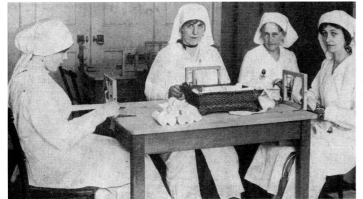

Women making bandages for injured troops. While their menfolk were away fighting, many women found themselves on the Home Front employed in useful tasks such as nursing, factory work, shell making and agricultural work.

A trip to Mount Edgcumbe was a popular pastime and many would visit the tearooms there. However, in August 1914 it was announced that the estate would be closed to the public due to the war until further notice.

Many men rush to enlist, 1914. As war was announced, men of all ages were keen to enlist and showed much patriotism. Many saw it as an adventure, a way to escape unemployment or their humdrum daily lives. Most thought that the war wouldn't last long and would be over by Christmas.

Kitchener's call to arms. The great numbers of men needed for the army were brought together by regular appeals by the authorities for young men to join up. The campaign went on around the country. This photo shows a recruitment speaker surrounded by flags and posters. On the chairs are the various uniforms of the army and the speaker is compelling young men to put one on rather than wearing civilian attire.

twelve hours. The newspapers reported that Plymouth was being used as England's principal base for military operations. The troops were assembled in Plymouth before being taken to Belgium to join the allied army. Thousands of troops were encamped at Plymouth ready for war duty.

Troop movement towards Plymouth began on 5 August and by 9 August, the British War Office had moved 120,000 men into the town.

The *Journal of Commerce* of 18 August reported:

The principal base of military operations is Plymouth, one of the most important of the southern shipping ports. There, the already perfected organization of the regular infantry and artillery branches of the service has been concentrating since the morning of August 5th.

During the day and night, more than 10,000 troops of these arms were assembled. The mobilization of these soldiers moved smoothly and within twenty-four hours, they were ready with full equipment for service.

The busy English seaport was transformed into an armed camp overnight. The railways there were virtually in possession of the Government that morning. Until August 9th, when our correspondent of the World left for New York, the regular schedules of train service between London and Plymouth were suspended, the Government assuming complete control.

The movement of troops and paraphernalia of war continued day and night without interruption from the morning of the fifth. In the four days from August 5th to August 9th, 120,000 British fighting men had been assembled at Plymouth, according to officers of the service to whom had been instructed the mobilization preliminary to the execution of plans for their transportation to Continental points.

The transportation began on August 7th, being conducted mainly at night and under the most rigid secrecy. Even the residents of the town were deprived of the opportunity to witness it at close range. The town was policed by territorial troops, organized for service at home, and to take the place of the regulars as they were sent away.

The military compelled the extinguishing of all lights throughout the town and particularly in that quarter facing the harbour.

On August 7th, eight cruisers and destroyers convoyed into Plymouth harbour, ten coastwise vessels and regular army vessels. These were anchored under the shelter of the forts at Drake's Island and Devonport, commanding the approaches to the harbour from the landing stages from which all civilians were strictly excluded.

Early in the morning of August 8th, the work of loading the regulars began. On the first three of the transports, field artillery and their crews were loaded. The other troop ships were given over to infantry. Just how many troops were sent on board three transports could not be learned, but the officers connected with that part of the service were making provisions for the dispatching of about 20,000 a day for several days.

French warships were seen outside the harbour of Plymouth during 7th, 8th and 9th August. It was the understanding that these vessels were to co-operate with the English warships in convoying the British troops to the Continental rendezvous agreed upon by France, England and Russia.

The belief was general among the officers who accompanied the first expeditions that their destination was to be some place in the North Sea, beyond the boundaries of neutral Holland.

On Saturday night, August 8th, and Sunday, August 9th, the advance guard of the cavalry service began to pour into Plymouth, together with trainload after trainload of quartermaster and commissary supplies, sufficient to care for a large army over several weeks, beside hospital corps and other paraphernalia of the campaign on foreign soil.

A feature of the latter equipment, was the assembling of 700 London motor buses which had been commandeered by the Government for field hospital service.

The make-up of the British fighting force sent to reinforce the Belgians and French, in Belgium under the command of Sir John French, is about as follows:

> *The field force comprises three army corps. Each of these includes two divisions and in addition, there is a cavalry division of uncertain proportions, which is commanded by Major-General Edmund Allenby.*

Twenty-four thousand men make up the infantry section of the army corps of Great Britain. It is divided into twenty-four infantry battalions, eighteen batteries of field artillery, two batteries of Howitzers or heavier guns and in addition, there are engineers, signal men, army service corps and other minor details.

As nearly as could be figured out, therefore, the British field force should consist of seventy-two infantry battalions, eighteen cavalry regiments, twenty-four batteries of horse drawn artillery (totalling 114 guns), fifty-four batteries of field artillery (324 guns) and six Howitzer batteries as well as the minor details.

Lieutenant General Sir Douglas Haig commands the first

army corps. The second was commanded by Lieutenant General Sir James Grierson, but he died suddenly yesterday, and will have to be replaced, and the third is led by Major-General W.P. Pulteney.

From the magnitude of the plans under way at Plymouth on August 9th, the despatching of England's contribution to the allied Continental armies opposing Germany was to be in full swing during the week that followed.

It was the belief of officers engaged in the service that more than 200,000 troops of all branches would be assembled at Plymouth during the week ending August 15th.

Meanwhile, in the same newspaper, Cunard were advertising luxury trips sailing from Montreal to Southampton stopping at Plymouth. Rates were $47.50 and up, while third class cost $30.25 and up.

On 13 August, Reverend W. Howard Coates, the vicar of Christ Church, Plymouth, introduced three new verses to the National Anthem that were sung on Sunday. These were:

Guard Thou his fleets at sea,
And may their colours be
Nailed to the mast
When fighting must be done,
May each Britannic son
Stand bravely by his gun,
True to the last.

What through the powers of hell,
Shelling o'er hill and dell,
Compass around
Raise him another Drake,
Who for his Monarch's sake
Each foeman's ship shall rake,
Ent'ring our Sound.

O Lord, Thou Prince of Peace,
Grant that ere long may cease
War's battle ring

Hasten the time, we pray,
When men no more shall slay,
And when all tongues shall say
God save the King!

A German was arrested at Runcorn on 24 August after posing as a British citizen. Karl Baker told authorities that he was born in Plymouth. However, he was registered as an alien in the town. He was charged with contravening the Aliens Registration Order by landing at a prohibited port after alighting from a boat in Runcorn docks.

On 26 August, Sergeant William Sutherland was killed at the Battle of Le Cateau.

He had formerly joined Plymouth Argyle as part of the reserve team and in 1911 was paid a signing fee of £100. He was unable to break into the Argyle first team and when war broke out he rejoined his old regiment, the Argyll and Sutherland Highlanders. He was killed just four days after the British Army first encountered the enemy.

William Sutherland joined Plymouth Argyle in 1911 and was paid a signing fee of £100. When war broke out he joined the Argyll and Sutherland Highlanders but was killed at the Battle of Le Cateau on 26 August 1914.

Also, on 26 August, twenty-six Belgian Reservists, officers and men arrived at Plymouth from the Congo before setting off to war.

On the same day, newspapers carried the story:

Law suit for over $1,000,000 in New York.
New York, Monday.
The Guaranty Trust Company have begun a law suit, involving over a million dollars, in connection with the failure of the German liner Kronprinzessen Cecilie to deliver several million dollars in gold at Plymouth in accordance with contract.

A telegram arrived at 1.15 am on Sunday 31 August for the Officer Commanding at Plymouth informing him that 120 wounded men would soon be arriving. An ambulance train arrived at Friary Station at 5 pm. On board were 100 weary and dusty men who had returned from fighting in northern France. They were transferred to the newly

Wounded troops returning from France in 1914. When the first wounded troops arrived on English soil from France, they were able to tell people about the war as it really was. It was said that anyone who met one of the wounded soldiers would never forget the emotions that it aroused.

converted hospital at Salisbury Road. In charge of the hospital were Lieutenant-Colonel H W Webber and Major J Cheyne Wilson. The soldiers were given a hot bath and chicken broth as well as much attention from the nursing staff.

The first shots by British troops on foreign soil took place on 21 August 1914. A military unit of the 4th Dragoon Guards, comprising 120 men, were sent on a reconnoitring mission ahead of the British Expeditionary Force. Although members of the British Expeditionary Force had landed a week before, no contact with the enemy had taken place. As forces advanced into France and Belgium, they heard stories from civilians that large numbers of German troops were advancing towards the town of Mons in Belgium. Shortly afterwards, the cavalry men of the Dragoon Guards encountered the enemy and the first shots taken in Europe since the Battle of Waterloo became the first of millions to be fired over the next four years.

On 2 September, Moses Russell made his first appearance for Plymouth Argyle in a match against Brighton and Hove Albion. The result for Plymouth was a 2 – 0 win. Although international football was suspended with the outbreak of war, the Southern League continued. Russell made twenty-five appearances with Argyle before play was suspended in 1915.

On 8 September, a chauffeur was shot by a sentry after failing to stop while driving a car bringing an officer back to Renney Fort. The bullet hit the chauffer in the right leg and he was taken to hospital. He was later named as Ernest Thorne, aged 19. Newspapers reported that: 'It was dark at the time he approached the fort and a high wind was blowing.'

On 10 September, Plymouth Argyle drew 2 – 2 against Brighton in the Southern League.

The *Evening Telegraph* of 10 September reported that the paymaster of the *Pathfinder* had been buried at Plymouth. The deceased, referred to only as 'Paymaster Finch', was picked up after the explosion but subsequently died of his injuries. His body had arrived in Plymouth the day before from

Moses Russell played most of his career for Plymouth Argyle. He was signed to the team in the summer of 1914 for a club record fee of £400. He made his debut in September 1914. He served as a private in the mechanised transport section of the Army Service Corps and was awarded the British War Medal and Victory Medal.

The Royal Naval Barracks, Devonport. Devonport was the base for the Western Approaches Squadron, which included some of the oldest battleships in service. Continued action against ships by German U-boats made the Devonport flotilla a vital necessity whose tasks included tracking down and either capturing or destroying the enemy submarines.

the north. The funeral party, including a band and gun carriage, was arranged by Devonport Naval Barracks. In attendance were a large amount of fellow officers. The *Pathfinder* had been sunk by a German submarine and approximately 250 of the crew were killed. Few lives were saved by British vessels who rushed to its aid.

On 11 September, it was reported in the *Coventry Evening Telegraph* that forty Germans who were considered too old to carry arms were being deported from Plymouth because the military authorities would prefer not to feed them for the duration of the war.

In September, the 2/5th (Prince of Wales') Battalion was formed in Plymouth as the Second Line Battalion. They would later become part of the 2nd Devon and Cornwall Brigade, 2nd Wessex Division.

On 17 September, the *Exeter and Plymouth Gazette* mentioned that they had received a letter from a detachment of marines who had passed through Exeter after leaving Plymouth. The letter said that they would like to thank the mayoress of Exeter and the people who passed them gifts on their way through Exeter station. They were quoted as saying 'the little packages were most acceptable.'

On 21 September, Cardinal Bourne arrived in Plymouth from Rome.

On 24 September, the crew of the cable steamer *Buccaneer* reached Plymouth safely after their vessel was lost at Tamatave in the Indian Ocean.

The *Western Times* of 24 September reported that the Sir Francis Drake bowls team from Plymouth had beaten Barnstaple in the Devon Rink Competition at Exeter. The score was 23 – 15.

On 25 September, the *Western Times* reported that Dr Mabel L. Ramsey of Plymouth was amongst a group of female English doctors whose offer of medical and surgical service had been accepted by the Allies. Dr Ramsey left for Antwerp on the previous Saturday to take charge of a hospital unit caring for wounded troops.

On 28 September, at Sandbach Sessions, John Goole, who was a private in the Special Reserve at Plymouth, was charged with being absent without leave. The authorities at Plymouth wired a Superintendent Sutton, who had apprehended Goole, requesting that he send the prisoner on without waiting for an escort. Goole promised to return if he was given a train ticket. The police had a collection so he would be able to buy refreshments on the journey back.

Wives wave off their loved ones as sailors leave on board a train. Most travelled third class and two men can be seen with pipes in the special 'smoking' carriage.

A horse being loaded on board ship. Hundreds of thousands of horses were requisitioned during the war and many died in combat. Some, however, did survive and were brought back to Britain and a few were cared for by animal charities.

In the *Western Times* of 29 September, it was reported that a Mrs M. Collins of Totnes had collected and forwarded 400 cigarettes to the men lying wounded at Salisury Road Hospital in Plymouth. The matron thanked her and stated: 'It is really good of you to think of the men here. Any little thing cheers them.'

The *Exeter and Plymouth Gazette* of 30 September carried a special announcement for the men of the 5th and 6th Devons. It read:

We have been asked to state, for the information of men on furlough, that trains returning to Ludgershall tomorrow, leave Plymouth (Friary) at 1.28 pm, Plymouth North Road at 2.50 pm and Torrington 3 pm.

An article in the *Exeter and Plymouth Gazette* of 2 October stated:

Corpl. Stoneman, of the Royal Field Artillery, 4nd Wessex Division, son of Sergt.-Instr. and Mrs Stoneman, of Whipton, has been selected to take a number of horses to France. Corpl. Stoneman, as well as his brothers, volunteered for active service. Jas. Stoneman is sailing for India with his Regiment. David, the youngest son, is stationed with the Engineers at Plymouth. Naturally, their parents are very proud of the patriotism of their sons.

A military church parade at Saltash. Hundreds of soldiers were stationed at Saltash and here they march by spectators, which include several enthralled children.

On 4 October, a military church parade, including locally stationed troops, took place at Saltash.

On 5 October, a huge fire engulfed the military hospital at Salisbury Road. Sick and wounded soldiers were quickly removed and all were saved.

On 8 October, the steamer *Nieuw Amsterdam*, part of the Holland-Amerika Line, arrived safely at Plymouth. The steamer had set sail on 29 September from New York and was diverted to Plymouth by the British authorities so that her cargo could be inspected.

On 8 October, a Private H.S. Elliott, RAMC, who was from Camborne but stationed in Plymouth, wrote to the *Cornishman* newspaper. His letter read:

> *I am writing you a few lines to let the people in Camborne know how the lads at Plymouth are getting along. We have the privilege, by the way, of reading your* Cornish Post *every week, which paper is appreciated by us who are a long way from home.*
>
> *We should like, if at all possible, for you to insert this letter in your paper.*
>
> *We are stationed at Eastern Kings, Stonehouse, Plymouth and are having a fine time.*
>
> *We get good food and are treated like gentlemen.*
>
> *We see lots of wounded soldiers brought in, including a good many Germans, and the latter are, in our opinion, a rough looking lot of fellows.*
>
> *I consider we are lucky to have such a fine time seeing the condition of the country at the present moment but, at the same time, we all trust the war will not be of long duration.*
>
> *We are all 'merry and bright', Mr Editor, as you will see by the report of Fun at the Fort which I append at foot. At the Fort on Friday evening last, I gave a recitation entitled The Footless Army, which recitation was taken from Mr Quintrell's book of poems. Mr Quintrell, as you know, lives at Wesley Street, Camborne.*

Below the letter was an article entitled *Fun at the Fort,* which read:

On Friday evening last, a smoking concert was held at Eastern Kings, Stonehouse, Plymouth by the men of the 2nd Relief 6th Company of the Devon R.G.A. During the evening, the following contributed to the programme: Bombardiers Harper and Johns, Gunners Chaffe, Lapthorne, Westcott, Carey, Ford, Clapp, Shelton, Hocking, Hopkins, Gunner S. Heath admirably presiding at the piano. Among the above contributions, a duet was given by Bombardiers Harper and Johns entitled You made me love you *and a song by Gunner Shelton entitled* I've got a motto *was received with great delight. Gunners Westcott and Bombardier Johns also received a great deal of applause after rendering their songs. A very pleasant evening was spent and terminating with singing* God save the King *and in giving three cheers for our brave lads at the front.*

On 9 October, 1/5th (Prince of Wales') Battalion of the Devonshire Regiment (Territorial Force stationed at Millbay) sailed for India.

The *Western Times* from 9 October reported that a train travelling between South Brent and Totnes had been fired upon. A Plymouth man, named only as 'Barker', reported that they were alarmed by a noise of

The 10th Battalion Lancashire Regiment were formed at Saltash in October 1914 as part of the 99th Brigade of the 33rd Division, which was a service battalion of the Fourth New Army.

something hitting the carriage. Both Barker and his companion looked out but saw nothing. Examination of the carriage later showed that it had indeed been struck as if hit by a bullet. The newspaper reported that 'the occurence remains a mystery'.

Reports on 10 October stated that the Antarctic Expedition steamer *Endurance*, which had previously left from Plymouth for Buenos Aires, had arrived safely in Monte Video.

In the *Western Times* of 10 October, Mortimer Brothers, the leading dyers and cleaners in Plymouth, announced that 'it was business as usual'. Their advert stated:

> *Although many of our workmen have been called up for active service, we have made complete arrangements for all orders to be executed with our usual promptness.*

On 10 October, in the *Exeter and Plymouth Gazette*, W. Howard Coates, the Vicar of Christ Church in Plymouth, suggested a new chorus to one of the troops' favourite songs. It read:

> *A la Tipperary.*
> *(With apologies to Jack Judge and Harry Williams)*
>
> *It's a long way to peace we long for,*
> *It's a long way to go;*
> *It's a long way to peace we pray for,*
> *To the sweetest gift below.*
> *Goodbye self-indulgence,*
> *Fairwell, soft armchair;*
> *It's a long, long way to peace we long for,*
> *But our heart's right there! It's a' there!*

On 12 October, Mr T. Baker was asked to become the first mayor of the new borough of Plymouth which now consisted of the Three Towns (Plymouth, Stonehouse and Devonport). He was already the Mayor of Plymouth before the amalgamation.

Also on 12 October, two sentries were mysteriously fired on at 9.30 pm in Plymouth. They were later admitted to hospital. The victims were privates in the Notts and Derby Regiment (the Sherwood Foresters).

Both had gunshot wounds to the legs. At first it was thought that they had been shot at from a passing train travelling over Laira railway bridge, which they were guarding, but it was later thought that the gunfire came from nearby bushes. Troops searched the area but found nothing. One of the sentries, Private Thomas Walter Smith, who was shot in the thigh, later died in hospital from his wound.

A report in the *Taunton Courier and Western Advertiser* of 14 October stated that police had detained seven deserters over the weekend in Taunton. Six of the men were detained at the Taunton Railway Station at 11.30 pm by PCs Giles and Hart. All were absentees from the 3rd Battalion of the South Staffs Regiment encamped at Staddon Heights in Plymouth. The seventh man detained was attached to X Company of the Worcester Regiment. All men were detained at the police station while awaiting escorts.

Schoolchildren cheering the fleet of transports on their arrival at Plymouth. The first contingent of Canadian troops arrived on 14 October 1914 and consisted of thirty-three liners carrying 25,000 Canadian volunteers.

On 14 October, thirty-three liners arrived in Plymouth Sound carrying 25,000 Canadian volunteers. The arrival was a complete surprise for the local authorities. Strict censorship meant that details of the Canadians arrival was kept secret from local authorities and residents.

The convoy had been due to land at Southampton but was diverted when news arrived that German submarines were waiting for them near the Solent.

Word soon got around of the arrival of the Canadian Armada and locals rushed to the Hoe and waterfront to cheer them.

People gathered to watch the Canadian troops disembark by the

The smiling faces of Canadian highlanders waving, on their way to camp in 1914 transported on an early motor bus. The hoarding on the side of the bus advertises My Lady's Dress, *the latest production at the local theatre.*

Millbay Skating Rink (which would later be the site of the Ballard Institute). As they disembarked they were given a warm welcome as they marched through the streets.

On 20 October, the troops paraded on Plymouth Hoe watched by local spectators.

Special trains waited for the troops at Millbay Station, who were carried aboard ninety-two trains while their vehicles were driven on by road. Onlookers remember their cheery, smiling faces as they waved towards them. It was probably seen as a great adventure for the soldiers, but many would later die at Vimy Ridge during April 1917. After leaving Plymouth, the Canadians occupied camps on Salisbury Plain before leaving for France. One of the troops, Major John McCrae, would later pen the words, '*In Flanders Fields the poppies blow, Between the crosses, row on row...*', which led to the poppy becoming the symbol of remembrance.

The Canadian troops parading on Plymouth Hoe in 1914. The troops arrived in Plymouth on 14 October. Over 25,000 volunteers arrived on thirty-three liners and were cheered on by locals who rushed to the Hoe to welcome them.

The departure of troops from Saltash on 22 October 1914. Saltash Passage in Plymouth can be seen in the background and this would be their destination after crossing the Tamar by ferry. They then marched to one of the nearby barracks before being sent to France.

The *Illustrated London News* reported:

On October 14th, the great armada that brought the Canadian Expeditionary Force reached Plymouth Hoe, that haven of heroic memory, whence the great Sir Francis Drake went to smash the 'Invincible Armada' of the Kaiser's prototype, Philip of Spain, who also dreamed of triumph over a prostrate England, and world of domination.

The Canadian contingent could be seen parading on the Hoe beside the Armada memorial together with Major-General E.A.H. Anderson who commands the Canadian contingent.

The enthusiasm with which the arrival of the Canadians was hailed by the 'Dogs of Devon' was a splendid echo of their own fine spirit in rushing to the defence of the Empire as soon as the news of war was flashed across the ocean.

On 22 October, troops left from Saltash crossing over the Tamar by ferry to Plymouth. Jubilant crowds cheered them on their way.

Canadian troops at Plymouth complete with their mascot, a parrot. The convoy had been due to land at Southampton but was diverted when news arrived that German submarines were waiting for them near the Solent. Word soon got around of the arrival of the Canadian Armada and locals rushed to the Hoe and waterfront to cheer them.

Canadian troops resting up at camp. By the end of the war Canadian casualties had numbered 215,000. A total of 600,000 Canadian soldiers had enlisted by 1918, which was approximately 13 per cent of the male population.

A photo carried in the paper showed men of the Canadian Expeditionary Force complete with their mascot, a parrot.

The *Graphic Newspaper*, published on 24 October, showed some Canadians posing for the camera, smiling and cheering, on board a motor bus on their way to camp.

Other newspapers also mentioned that the cavalry and infantry were in jovial spirits and sang as they marched. Crowds lined the streets and cheered them on as they passed. On train platforms, as they prepared to leave Plymouth, troops and civilians sang patriotic songs including 'It's a long way to Tipperary'.

In the *Saskatoon Star, Phoenix* of 29 July 1964, the event was remembered fifty years later:

> *Fifty years ago this summer, Canada went to war with singing in the streets.*
>
> *A nation of barely more than 7,000,000, insignificant as a military power, plunged into the First World War in 1914 on an upswelling of patriotism and enthusiasm that was almost carnival.*
>
> *Within hours, thousands of men were clamoring to be recruited. There was betting that the war wouldn't last until the end of the year. Fear was expressed publicly that Canadians wouldn't have a chance to get into the fighting.*

Only a handful guessed at the horrors that lay ahead.

Formal word of war arrived at 8.55 p.m. on the warm Tuesday evening of August 4th when a cable from the British government was delivered to the Duke of Connaught, then Governor-General, in session with Prime Minister, Robert Borden and his cabinet.

It reported tersely that Britain – and its Empire – had declared war on the Kaiser's Germany.

As the news spread across the land, parades and demonstrations erupted in cities, towns and villages.

Crowds jammed downtown Montreal La Marseillaise and sang Rule Britannia. *In Toronto, 2,000 volunteers marched along Yonge Street behind a fife-and-drum band. The Governor-General's Foot Guards paraded 350 strong in Ottawa led by three bands and cheered by 15,000 onlookers.*

Nobody questioned the fact that Canada was at war.

Four years earlier, Sir Wilfrid Laurier, then prime minister, had stated it plainly in the house of commons:

'When Britain is at war. Canada is at war. There is no distinction.'

Borden, the opposition leader, had warmly supported that stand.

But 1914 was a situation never to be repeated. The Statute of Westminster, 17 years later, gave Canada her own voice in the world and the right to decide for herself whether and when to go to war.

In 1939, Canada's parliament voted to enter the Second World War a week after Britain's decision.

Late on the night of August 4th, 1914, reports of the patriotic displays poured into Ottawa from every corner of the nation.

The Governor-General cabled London:

Great exhibition of patriotism here. When inevitable fact transpires that considerable period of training will be necessary before Canadian troops will be fit for European war this ardor is bound to be dampened somewhat. In order to minimize this, I would suggest that any proposal from you should be accompanied by the assurance that Canadian troops will go to the front as soon as they have reached a sufficient standard of training.

The Duke was right. Within 48 hours, the initial reaction was over, but it was replaced by a grim determination that Canada would play its full role in the struggle.

There had been some preparation but not much. The actual outbreak of war jolted most Canadians, who had been watching the storm clouds gather over Europe for so long that it no longer seemed important.

Only 10 days before, not one major newspaper in the country had carried a front-page story about the mounting crisis. Most of them played up the famous Paris trial of Henriette Caillaux who had shot to death the editor of Figaro for accusations of treason against her husband, an ex-premier of France. It was a real sizzler.

Borden wrote in his memoirs 20 years later: ' Although the events had quite prepared us for this result, it came at the last as a shock. None of us at that time anticipated the terrible duration of the war agony.'

Compared to the great powers, Canada had a small, obsolete military force. The authorized permanent army was 3,110 men and 684 horses, mainly engaged in garrison duty and the training of the militia, which had an authorized force of 70,000 men and 16,700 horses. Neither was up to strength.

There were 200 artillery pieces, almost no transport, two cast-off British cruisers used as training ships and no air force.

It was a motley collection, and why not? Canada's main international event of 1914 was the celebration of 100 years of peace with the United States.

The first actions of the Canadian cabinet were to call Parliament into session for August 18th and offer Britain a gift of 98,000,000 pounds of flour, an offer quickly accepted.

Parliament voted $50,000,000 for war costs and approved the initial plan to send a 20,000-man army force to France.

There wasn't even a hint that the war was eventually to cost Canada 35 times that amount of money and put 600,000 men

The Canadian Contingent in Europe. The Contingent, who had arrived at Plymouth in the autumn of 1914, found themselves in Flanders by December of that year. Their caps bore the Maple Leaf badge.

and women into uniform. Nor that 426,500 would cross the Atlantic, one in three to be wounded and one in seven to die.

The war's first real impact on the country was the departure of thousands of British, French and Belgian reservists. Almost everyone had a neighbour who left to answer the mobilization call from his European homeland.

On August 6th, the call went out from Ottawa for recruits to gather at Valcartier, a new training camp hacked out of the bush, 16 miles northwest of Quebec City. Within a month 100 special trains had poured 32,665 volunteers into the camp.

Creation of Valcartier almost overnight was a spectacular triumph engineered by Sir Sam Hughes, the minister of militia in Borden's cabinet and one of the most erratic and controversial figures of the war.

Training was rigorous and intense consisting mainly of rifle and machine-gun practice.

'I want first of all, men who can pink the enemy every time,' Sir Sam told his troops in one of his many speeches, often delivered from horseback as he rode proudly about the campsite.

He boasted that the men at Valcartier had been 'trained to handle a rifle as no men had ever handled it before.'

The rifle involved was the Ross, a story in itself. It was produced in Canada by the Scottish industrialist, Sir Charles Ross under a contract signed by the Laurier government. Eventually the army was to have 342,000 of them.

Despite its political ancestry, Sir Sam put up an almost pathological defence of the Ross rifle when it came under severe criticism a year later. It was an efficient target weapon but jammed under heavy use. Canadian troops in battle began throwing it away to pick up the hardy Lee-Enfields from fallen British soldiers. Yet it wasn't discarded until mid-1916.

During the Valcartier training period, the original target of 20,000 men for the first overseas contingent was boosted to 25,000 and – almost at the last minute – to 30,000.

After a nightmarish loading operation, the flotilla of 30 transports carrying 30,621 men, their horses and equipment, sailed from Gaspe Harbor on Oct. 2. It arrived safely at Plymouth after a smooth 12-day crossing, guarded by a Royal Navy battle fleet.

It wasn't the first Canadian unit to reach England, however. That distinction went to the Princess Patricia's Canadian Light Infantry, a regiment formed by veterans of the South African war who came from all parts of Canada. The Patricia's were organized under the initiative of Capt. A. Hamilton Gault of Montreal, himself a South African veteran who put up $100,000 of the cost, and were named for the Governor-General's daughter.

The Patricia's reached England in late September and went into the front line the night of January 6th-7th, 1915. This unit was almost wiped out in a German attack in 1916.

Arrival of the main Canadian body, however, touched off a celebration in Plymouth with cheers, kisses, cigarettes and drinks. It was the first major contingent to reach Britain from her overseas Dominions and Winston Churchill, then first lord of the admiralty, cabled Ottawa:

'Canada sends her aid at a timely moment'.

The cheerful arrival did nothing to prepare the Canadians for the shock ahead. They were taken by train to a camp on

Salisbury Plain, there to spend 18 weeks in mud, rain, cold and lice. It rained on 89 of the next 123 days, soaking the light tents and everything in them. Mud seeped through blankets and kits.

Adding to the discomfort wa Sir Sam's edict against wet canteens. It was rescinded only after heavy pressure from Gen. E. A. H. Alderson, commander of the 1st Canadian Division, and despite protests from temperance organizations back home.

A mistaken sense of relief swept the ranks when the orders came to move out to France. The division disembarked at St. Nazaire on February 15th and late on the afternoon of March 3rd took over 4,000 yards of front between Bois-Grenier and Armentieres, in northern France near the Belgian border.

The Canadians had one quiet week to adapt themselves to the routine of trench warfare. Then all hell broke loose. The war had waited for them after all, and it was far from over.

Injured troops prepare to return home. In the first year of the war there were very few hospital trains equipped for the needs of wounded soldiers. Third-class trains were used and wounded and gassed soldiers would have to sit upright on the long journey. Special hospital trains were later introduced.

Walking wounded and bedraggled troops wait to board a train to take them to hospital. All are dishevelled and dirty from fighting at the Front. Carriages in the background are packed with soldiers taking a break for refreshments before returning to a rest camp.

On 17 October, a large number of wounded men arrived in Southampton straight from the Front. They were sent on to various locations around Britain including Glasgow, Aberdeen, Netley, Leicester, London and Plymouth.

On 18 October, it was reported that the steamship *Dorie* had arrived at Plymouth carrying 6,000 tons of provisions provided by the Canadian government to aid destitute Belgians in Holland and Belgium. The steamer had travelled from Halifax in Nova Scotia.

As wounded soldiers returned to Plymouth by train, children rushed up to North Road Station to watch them arrive. Endless troops returned on special hospital trains. Some were walking with the aid of crutches while many others, with terrible injuries, were carried on stretchers. They were taken to the nearby military hospitals.

During school lessons, teachers gave their classes the latest updates on the war including any victories or defeats.

On 22 October, a German spy was shot at Plymouth. Mr R.W. Gray, who was a coal agent in Dundee, had two sons in the Canadian contingent who had recently arrived in Plymouth. One of his sons wrote a letter to him saying:

One of our volunteers was shot at Plymouth. He had three or four pounds of dynamite on him and was proved to be a German spy. I suppose he was up to mischief of some kind.

Entertainment still carried on in Plymouth. On 23rd October, the *Evening News* reported that:

> *Arthur Pelkey, the heavyweight of Chicopee, Massachusetts, who is still in England, won a battle at Plymouth a few nights ago by knocking out Frank Hagney of Australia in five rounds. Hagney could not have been much when he allowed a man like Pelkey to stop him.*

The fight took place at the Cosmopolitan Gymnasium in Mill Street, Devonport where Pelkey would later win a fight against Harry Smith on 13 November. Arthur Pelkey was born in Canada in 1884 and fought in matches between 1910 and 1920. On 24 May 1913, Pelkey fought Luther McCarty at *Tommy Burn's Arena* in Calgary, Alberta. Two minutes into the first round, Pelkey knocked out McCarty and McCarty died eight minutes later. Pelkey was cleared of killing McCarty and the death was put down to injury in a previous boxing match. However, the legal proceedings bankrupted Pelkey and he was never the same man again.

C. W. Trace of 94 Treville Street published a postcard in 1914 with the title *Europe's Cock Robin*, which showed a bird with the head of the Kaiser. The card read:

Arthur Pelkey was a boxer who was born in Canada in 1884 and fought in matches between 1910 and 1920. During October 1914 he fought Frank Hagney of Australia at the Cosmopolitan Gymnasium in Mill Street, Devonport. Pelkey knocked out Hagney after five rounds.

> *Who'll kill old Kaiser Bill?*
> *We! Says France, England. Belgium and Russia,*
> *We'll make him wish he never knew Prussia,*
> *The murdering blackguard, Kaiser Bill.*
>
> *Who'd like to see him die?*
> *We! Cries aloud the civilised world,*
> *In a fiery furnace he ought to be hurled,*

We'd coolly stand by and see him die.
Who'll make his shroud?
He shouldn't have one, let him die like a rat,
It would only be giving back tit for tat,
We'd watch making him a shroud.

Who'll carry him to his grave?
No one would do it, is the people's reply,
We'll drag him there naked instead is the cry.
Fancy, carrying Kaiser Bill to his grave.

Who'll be chief mourner?
No one, they'd surely expect to be shot,
To mourn for him would be all tommy rot.
Sounds like a joke to ask, who'll be chief mourner?

Who'll toll the bell?
Everybody. Old men and woman would want a pull,
Each feeling armed with the strength of a bull.
Don't you fancy you hear the bell toll?

Not a sound would be heard of sighing or of sobbing,
When we hear of the death of Europe's Cock Robin.

An advert in the *Cornishman* of Thursday 24 October announced:

War Prices – you can furnish cheaply now. To keep hands employed,
Snawdon's are selling at great sacrifices. Cost prices, practically.
Why not investigate? It pays. Write for lists – The Mart, Plymouth.

Further down the column was another advert that read:

Ladies! Do not dispair!! Rogers pills never fail!!! 1s., 2s. 6d., 4s.
6d. 10s 6d. Strongest 21s. Post free anywhere – Rogers'
Pharmacy, 128 Exeter Street, Plymouth. Mention this newspaper.

On 29 October, it was reported that Captain John Jacob Astor had been
wounded in battle. He was the brother of the Member of Parliament

for Plymouth, Waldorf Astor.

On 30 October, the captains of nine captured German liners arrived at Plymouth and were held as prisoners of war.

Also on 30 October, Lord Henry Seymour arrived at Plymouth. He had been wounded in the fighting at the Cameroons.

When, on 31 October, the English barque *Gladys* arrived at Plymouth, several members of her crew were arrested because they were of German nationality. They were classed as prisoners of war. The journey to Plymouth had been a rough one. Horace Newcombe Tansley, the second officer, was swept overboard and drowned in gales off Cape Horn.

On 1 November, the P&O steamer *Malojay* landed at Plymouth carrying survivors whose vessels had come under attack from the German cruiser *Emden*. The survivors included Captain W. H. Gibson of the London steamer *Foyle* and Captain Harris of the London steamer *King Lud*. The steamers were sunk by *Emden* near the Laccadive Islands in the Indian Ocean in September. The crew were landed at Columbo.

In November, America sent a ship full of Christmas gifts for war orphans in Plymouth. American newspapers reported on 26 November that the *Santa Claus Ship* was met with much joy and that Plymouth

The SMS Emden *sank or captured thirty Allied warships and merchant vessels in the early part of the war. She became the most hunted German vessel and was finally brought to an end by HMAS* Sydney. *In the battle that ensued, 131 German personnel were killed and sixty-five wounded. Captain von Müller beached the vessel on North Keeling Island and the surviving crew were later made prisoners of war.*

The USS Jason *at Devonport. On Wednesday 25 November 1914, the USS* Jason *was met at the Eddystone by a destroyer flotilla. Cordial greetings were exchanged before the ship landed at Devonport. The cargo included many gifts in 2,000 packing cases, which weighed a total of 8,000 tons.*

and Devonport had been festooned with decorations to welcome the Americans. Huge crowds gathered to welcome the *Jason* as warships directed it into the harbour. Lord Kitchener sent a message expressing the army's gratitude, which was read at a banquet for the ship's officers.

The ship was loaded with 8,000 tons of gifts comprising 5,000,000 separate articles that had been donated by American children and were destined for British, Belgian, French, German and Austrian children whose fathers were away fighting in the war.

The ship was officially welcomed by Earl Beauchamp, the president of the council, on behalf of the government. He was accompanied by Mr F. D. Acland, the Under-Secretary of Foreign Affairs, together with a large gathering of naval and military officers.

Among the greetings awaiting the ship was one from the queen to the wife of the American ambassador. In her letter, the queen wrote:

> *I am anxious to express through you my warm appreciation of this touching proof of generosity and sympathy and to ask you to be so kind as to convey my heartfelt thanks to all who have contributed towards these presents, which will, I am sure, be gladly welcomed by the children for whom they are intended and*

received with gratitude by their parents.
The scheme was initiated by the *Chicago Herald* and a Mr O'Loughlin, who represented the journal, stated that 200 other newspapers throughout the United States had assisted in the project. As well as an enormous collection of toys, gifts also included shoes, boots, clothing, sweaters and stockings. So much was collected that 100,000 tons of presents had to be left behind.

While the *Jason* was at Plymouth, gifts were left for British and Belgian children before the ship carried on its journey to Marsailles to deliver presents to German children. It then carried on to Genoa to distribute gifts to further German and Austrian children. Gifts heading for Russia were loaded on to a different vessel.

On 9 November, the Workers' National Committee and London Trades Council proposed that soldiers and sailors should receive £1 a week out of public funds for wives of privates, and five shillings for every child under 16. They proposed that £1 a week should be paid to disabled servicemen for the length of their incapacity. They also proposed pensions for wives of servicemen who lose their lives.

Mr Ben Tillett at Plymouth stated:

If the Government met their demands, they would within the next month, be able to command a million men of the finest fighting type in the world. Without concessions they could expect no help from Labour organizations. If they threatened conscription, a national strike might follow.

On 9 November, the steamer *Itaban* arrived in Plymouth. On board were seventeen officers and crew of the Dutch steamer *Maris*, which had been sunk by the German cruiser *Karlsruhe*. On board had been 23,000 quarters of wheat that were bound for Belfast.

On 10 November, the death was announced, in the *Western Daily Press*, of Captain Percy Vaughan Lewis, CB, DSO at the Royal Naval Hospital in Plymouth. Captain Vaughan Lewis had been invalided home from the *Superb*, which was under his command. He was 49 years old.

On 11 November, 1/5th (Prince of Wales') Battalion (Devonshire Regiment Territorials) landed at Karachi where they came under the command of the 3rd (Lahore) Divisional Area at Multan.

The *Aberdeen Journal* of 14 November reported that a verdict of suicide had been recorded, at an inquest in Plymouth, concerning the death on the previous Wednesday of Lieutenant-Quartermaster Sidney Fielding. He was attached to the 3rd Battalion Notts and Derbyshire Regiment stationed at Crownhill. He had been found shot in the head, with a revolver at his side at the barracks. He regained consciousness in hospital but made no reference to the matter. He later died. His brother stated that the deceased was 'of a singularly happy disposition.'

On 16 November, Spooners in Plymouth announced that they had a sale on with stock being provided by E. Paul and Sons of Penzance.

On 17 November, the 3rd Battalion of the Kings Own Royal Lancashire Regiment, who were camped at Wearde near Saltash, left by ferry for the short journey over to Plymouth. Crowds gathered to watch them leave but there was a more sombre mood than there had been a month earlier.

On 21 November, under the 'Auction' section of the *Western Times*, a sale was announced that consisted of goods from the *Schlesien* and other naval prizes. Some of the contents listed included: 328 bags of white pepper, sixty-five bags of rice, fifty-five bags of cinnamon bark,

The troops stationed at Weard near Saltash. The 3rd Battalion of the King's Own Royal Lancaster Regiment were based in fields between Cross Park and Wearde Farm near Saltash at the beginning of the war. The camp included hundreds of tents but plans were soon made for more permanent structures comprising wooden huts.

Troops board the Saltash ferry to travel to Plymouth. On 17 November 1914, the 3rd Battalion of the King's Own Royal Lancashire Regiment left Saltash for Plymouth. They were waved off by a large crowd as they left on the ferry to cross the Tamar River. They had previously arrived in Saltash in August 1914 and had camped at Weard.

100 cases of sticklac, forty-five bales of hemp tow, four bags M of P shells, feathers, 7 tons of buffalo horns, gambege, sixty 'Calmon' motor tyres, fifty-four cases of gum damar, sixteen barrels of salted beef and pork and general ships' stores.

The auction was held by Robert Lyon and Co and commenced at 12 noon on Friday 27 November.

On 22 November, the P&O steamer *India* arrived at Plymouth from Gibraltar. On board were eight officers and crew of the *Benmohr*, which had been sunk by the German cruiser *Emden*, on 16 October. The *Benmohr* was reported to have been carrying a valuable cargo from London to Penang when it was sunk.

On 23 November, Major-General A.P. Penton, in charge of the Plymouth Fortress, requested that all houses that faced seawards should have their windows blacked out at night.

On 24 November, the *Hull Daily Mail* reported that there were 2,955 aliens permitted in prohibited areas. This included three males and five females in Plymouth and Devonport.

On 25 November, a Samuel Stubbs appeared in court in Derby charged with being a deserter from the 1st Battalion Notts and Derby

Regiment stationed at Plymouth. The defendant was said to be 'shaking like a leaf'. The prisoner admitted desertion but said that the reason was that he wanted to visit his wounded brother. He stated that he had joined up in 1905 and had served with the colours for nine years before being placed on reserve. He requested some quinine tablets to treat the malaria he'd picked up in India, which was the cause of his shaking. He was remanded while he awaited an escort.

On 1 December, it was reported that a second battalion of the 5th Devon Territorials would not be sent to India at the present time after the order to send 350 more men was cancelled by the War Office. Recruiting for the unit continued and it was stated that men would be dispatched to India when needed.

The *Exeter and Plymouth Gazette* of 3 December reported that a third person had died resulting from a tramcar accident that had taken place on 27 November. The accident had taken place at Devonport and the deceased was named as Robert D. Ford, a labourer, of 46 Richmond

A Zeppelin preparing for flight. With the outbreak of war, Germany made great use of Zeppelins for reconnaissance and bombing raids. In 1910 they were first flown commercially by Deutsche Luftschiffahrts-AG (DELAG) and by 1914 they had carried 34.000 pasengers on 1,500 separate flights.

Street. He died of his injuries in hospital.

On 5 December, the Glasgow steamer *Cloch* arrived in Plymouth. On board were three survivors from the steamer *Waterloo*, which foundered off the Lizard. A total of fourteen lives were lost, including the captain. The three saved were the chief engineer, the mate and the boatswain, who were rescued after clinging to the wreckage in the water for two to three hours.

The *Manchester Evening News* announced on 9 December that, despite the war, the P&O steamer *Kaisar-i-hind* had completed a record journey from Plymouth to Bombay taking seventeen days, twenty hours and fifty-two minutes.

The *Fielding Star* from 10 of December reported that:

> *A gentleman in Berlin, writing to his German daughter in Torquay, expresses fears for her safety, as the Berlin papers state that London and Plymouth have been practically destroyed by fires caused by Zeppelin bombs.*
>
> *He writes:*
>
> *'We have confidence in our grand army. We are thankful that our country has been spared from seeing the war. London must be awful. Half burnt down and Zeppelins always hovering over the place. Two years ago, we spent such a pleasant time in the beautiful city and now it has been almost destroyed.*
>
> *We have been told that Plymouth has also been destroyed by fire. I believe that you are near Plymouth. I pray that you are safe'.*
>
> *He adds that in the German capital many dogs are being destroyed in order that they shall not encroach on the food supplies of the people.*
>
> *He also writes:*
>
> *'I suppose it will soon be over, as England cannot find the money to continue the war.'*

The same newspaper stated:

> *Wealthy Germans are making their way out of their own country by any and every route that is open, and are getting away just*

Devonport Drillers on war service in Gibraltar. Gibraltar's dockyard and naval base played a vital role in the First World War and was Britain's principal base in the western Mediterranean.

as fast as they can travel. Algeciras, Malaga and other towns in the south of Spain (says a private letter from Gibraltar) are full of millionaire manufacturers, merchants and financiers from the Fatherland and their number is swelling everyday.

On 11 December, a letter from Horace Lincoln, a Bedfordshire artilleryman, was published in the Luton Times and Advertiser. It read:

We left Bombay in 62 troop ships, 50 of which left us at Gibraltar for Northern France, the remaining 12 proceeding to Plymouth, where we landed. We were escorted by 12 cruisers. Troop ships and cruisers travelled throughout the nights with lights out. There are 12,000 troops in this camp, all from India. We are staying here for about 5 weeks and then we leave for the Front.

On 13 December, Plymouth entertained the chess championships competing against Torquay.

On 14 December, the *Western Morning News* published the statement, 'The Admiralty have intimated that separating allowances are not to be paid to the widows of naval men for six months after the husband's death, as in the case with widows of army men.'

The *Exeter and Plymouth Gazette* of Tuesday 15 December carried a photo of the late Sergeant G.T. White, who was a member of the 1st Devons and was killed in action at Festubert on 30 October. He had formerly played for the Exeter FC Reserves and had been the captain of the Plymouth and District League team.

In December, the MP for Brentford, William Johnson-Hicks, had the idea to form the 'Footballers' Battalion', the 17th Service Battalion of the Middlesex Regiment. There were already many local 'Pals' regiments around the country and battalions featuring sportsmen seemed a good idea. The Saracens and Wasps announced that 98 per cent of their players had joined the 'Rugby Battalion'. However, the Footballers' Battalion had a very limited take-up. From eleven Lancashire football clubs, only forty players had joined up.

By the end of November, eleven players from Argyle had joined the army and recruitment gathered pace. Of the 5,000 professional football players in Britain, 2,000 joined up and approximately 600 were killed in battle.

On 17 December, the captured German ship *Melpomene* made its way towards Plymouth being towed by the tug *Hotspur*. It had been captured by an HM cruiser with a cargo of nitrate. It had previously been detained at Queenstown as a war prize.

On 18 December, a contingent of 900 Australian reservists from 131 different regiments arrived in Plymouth. The *Dundee Courier* stated: 'They are a fine body of men and will show the Kaiser the fighting qualities of the

Sergeant G.T. White was a member of the 1st Devons and was killed in action at Festubert on 30 October. He had formerly played football for Exeter FC Reserves as well as being the captain of the Plymouth and District League team.

Septimus Atterbury made eighty-eight appearances in the football league playing for Plymouth Argyle, Barnsley, Leicester Fosse and Loughborough. He also made 410 appearances in the Southern League. He joined Argyle in 1907 and continued to play for them until 1921. During the war years he played for Leicester Fosse as a wartime guest.

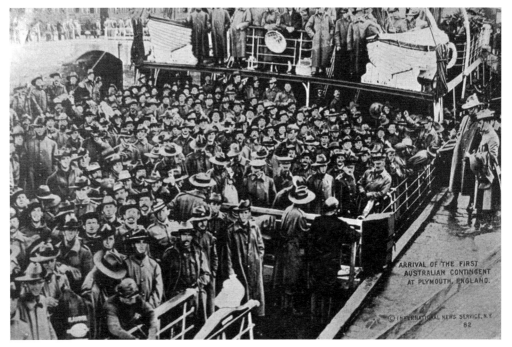

The arrival of the first Australian Contingent at Plymouth. Thousands of troops from overseas arrived at Plymouth during December 1914. They played a vital part during the war effort.

inhabitants of the colonies he covets.'

Also on 18 December, two men drowned at Devonport Dockyard. William John Beer, aged 31, of Oakfield Terrace, and Archibald Charles Penrose of Valletort Place, Devonport, lost their lives when a boat in which the men were working was dragged underwater by the suction of propellers on a nearby warship. A third man was rescued safely.

On 22 December, a train carrying seventy wounded soldiers to Plymouth passed through Exeter where members of the Exeter Voluntary Aid Detachment waited for them on the platform. The soldiers were provided with refreshments and it was reported that 'there were very few serious cases'.

Many troops spent Christmas in Europe with gifts and cards from loved ones and well-wishers.

On 28 December, it was reported that the quartermaster-general for the Plymouth Fortress, a Major R.F. Lock, was thrown from his horse while riding at Devonport. The horse ran off down a steep hill before crashing through a fence. Major Lock received nasty injuries to his

Delivery of Christmas fund gifts 1914. Christmas gifts meant a lot to the men at the Front and many were sent to the troops overseas from Britain. Here members of the Army Veterinary Corps are seen receiving their share.

Christmas at the Front 1914. British soldiers found many a sprig of mistletoe amongst the apple trees spread throughout the orchards of France. Here the troops celebrate on top of a captured German gun.

Christmas 1914 complete with a Christmas tree and cards. The king and queen requested that all men serving abroad should receive a Christmas card from them and the photo shows them being handed out. In the background is a makeshift Christmas tree decorated with whatever could be found.

A soldier receives a Christmas gift from home. Many soldiers received a special Christmas gift from the HRH Princess Mary's Gift Fund during Christmas 1914. Here a corporal receives a parcel containing cigarettes and tobacco. Throughout the war families sent regular packages to their troops at the Front, which included food and clothing.

head, legs and face.

On 30 December, 635 prisoners of war, including Germans, were landed at Plymouth. Many of the prisoners came from Gibraltar and the West Coast of Africa and included sixty-five officers, fifty-seven Turkish subjects as well as a number of Austrians. Two trains were requisitioned to take them to the quarters where they would be detained.

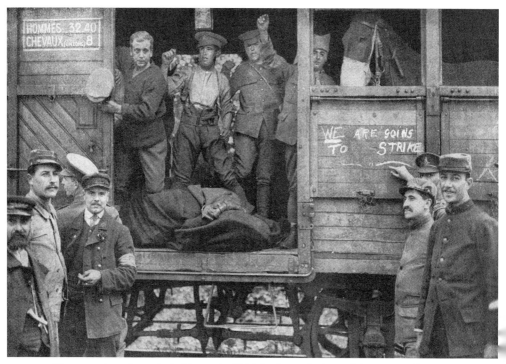

Troops on board a train in France in 1914. In the early days of the war much strain was put on the railway service in France as every bit of rolling stock was brought into use for the transportation of troops. The carriage shown is marked '8 horses and 32 to 40 men', showing the coach's capacity.

CHAPTER 2

1915
Deepening Conflict

The *Exeter and Plymouth Gazette* of 1 January carried a story about the Christmas gifts that had arrived from America. It read:

> *All recognise the goodwill that prompted our American cousins to send a Santa Claus ship to Europe for the benefit of the little ones of the various nations, whose fathers are engaged in the*

The *USS* Jason, *which was known as the Santa Claus Ship. The ship brought gifts from America to the orphaned children of servicemen serving in Europe. Huge crowds gathered to welcome the* Jason *as warships directed it into the harbour. Lord Kitchener sent a message expressing the army's gratitude, which was read at a banquet to the ship's officers.*

*war. But, unfortunately, when the cargo for England, unloaded
at Plymouth by the* Jason, *was unpacked, it was quickly seen that
there would be by no means sufficient presents for children in
the United Kingdom whose fathers had been killed at the front
or are at present fighting. Exeter's share of the cargo arrived in
the city four days before Christmas and consisted of three cases.
When these were unpacked, they were found but to contain a
very limited number of toys, the rest, for the most part, being
clothing, chiefly adult, some new but the majority second-hand.
In addition, there were some packets of nuts etc.*

On 11 January, it was reported that the German barque
Vizanella, with a valuable nitrate cargo, was brought to
Plymouth. The same article mentioned that the Industrial
Life Assurance offices had already paid £225,000 on
11,000 claims for soldiers and sailors killed in the war.

In January, 1915, a story published in *The Times* read:

*More than 200 recruits have been enrolled in London
for the Football Battalion of the Middlesex Regiment,
in addition to 400 from other districts. Among the
recruits are several rugby international players of
England, Ireland and Scotland, and the officers
include more than one Double Blue. The commanding
officer is Colonel C F Grantham, late of the Indian
Army, and commissions have been given among others
to Vivian J Woodward and Evelyn H Lintott, two well
known players.*

*Evelyn Lintott,
footballer and officer,
was killed on the first
day of the Battle of the
Somme. He played for
Plymouth Argyle as
well as Queen's Park
Rangers before the
outbreak of war. He
was one of the first
players to sign up for
the army in 1914 and
enlisted with the Leeds
Pals (West Yorkshire
Regiment's 15th
Battalion).*

On 20 January, a Mrs Moore of Torrington Place,
celebrated her 104th birthday, making her the oldest
resident in Plymouth.

Newspapers during January reported the rising cost of
food in Plymouth. The price of bread, which was 7d a
loaf, was the highest since the American-Spanish war. Wheat prices
were at their highest ever.

The 33rd battery Canadian Field Artillery left Toronto during
January and arrived at Plymouth three weeks later. From there they

A local football team. Although international football was suspended with the outbreak of war, the Southern League continued. Criticism of football was voiced locally because of the three towns' strong military tradition. Local newspapers stopped reporting on match results so they could include page after page of those wounded or killed in battle.

camped in England before setting off for Le Harve in France. They were then sent direct to the battlefront around Ypres for three months before being transferred to the Somme.

On 3 February, the *Western Daily Press* reported of a recent tramway fatality at Tamar Terrace, Devonport. The government inspector stated that the primary cause of the accident was the motorman exceeding the proper speed along Tamar Terrace, which caused the wheels to jam. The tramcar had accommodation for forty-six passengers, although sixty-six were actually on board at the time. The overcrowding was seen to be a factor in the accident but the inspector stated that 'the fault must also lie with the passengers who insist on getting onto a full tramcar whilst the conductor is helpless to stop them.'

During February, the revue *Business as Usual* began its tour of England at Plymouth and had previously been hugely successful at the Hippodrome in London. The *Cornishman* Newspaper reported that the show 'deals with the passing war spirit, has many catchy tunes and finishes with a grand march of the Allies.'

On 6 February, battalions of Plymouth and Chatham were moved by train from Shillingstone, near Blandford, to Devonport. They were

Soldiers of the 2nd battalion of the Devonshire regiment, No.4 Section, 'F' Company at Stonehouse Barracks. The barracks have housed members of the Royal Marines since the 1780s.

temporarily known as the Royal Marine Special Service Force. At 6 pm on the same day, the Plymouth Battalion together with the headquarters of the Royal Marine Brigade set sail for Malta on board the *Braemar Castle*. They arrived at St Paul's Bay in Malta on 14 February before continuing on their journey on the 19th. After passing through Tenedos they arrived at Dardanelles on 26 February before returning back to Tenedos. A planned landing at Gallipoli on 28 February was abandoned due to bad weather.

The *Illustrated War News* of 10 February showed a photo of Vice-Admiral Sir Doveton Sturdee at Admiralty House, Plymouth.

The story read:

Vice-Admiral Sir Doveton Sturdee, who commanded the British squadron in the victory off the Falkland Islands, recently landed at Plymouth. On the 3rd, he came up to London, were he was received by the King, and called at the Admiralty. When he reached his home in Droxford, Hampshire, the next day, he had a great reception. The village was en fete and the inhabitants took the horses from the carriage and drew it to the Admiral's house, preceded by a brass band. In replying to a speech of welcome, Sir Doveton Sturdee said that he thought many more men might be needed for the British forces before the war ended.

On 22 February, the *Western Daily Mercury*, published in Plymouth, reported that the Australian mail boat *Maloja* was seen entering the English Channel on Saturday morning. Also on board were 400 passengers. The *Maloja* was ordered to stop by an armed merchant vessel. As no identification could be seen on the approaching vessel, the *Maloja* decided to take no risks and continued on its journey without stopping.

Her speed was brought up to 20 knots as she headed towards Plymouth. The merchant vessel fired a blank shot before firing live shells. Luckily, all shells fell short of the mail boat and it was later accompanied to Plymouth by a patrol boat.

At the beginning of March, many newspapers criticised America for their neutrality.

Admiral of the Fleet Sir Frederick Charles Doveton Sturdee. Sturdee commanded the British squadron in the victory off the Falkland Islands. On 8 December 1914, whilst taking on coal at Stanley, he came under attack from German cruisers. Sturdee's forces managed to sink all of the ships apart from the light cruiser Dresden, *which was tracked down some months later.*

The *Western Morning News* in Plymouth reported:

If Americans were in our position they would act precisely as we have done, and might well have improved upon it, at least, in the matter of time. As neutrals they would naturally like to get the best of both worlds, but when the Germans threaten the Americans as well as the British with assassination and pillage on the high seas, the alternative we offer them is at least tempered by mercy and justice. If their goods escape the German torpedoes or are seized or held up by the Allies, they will receive ample compensation. We sympathize with the neutrals but our consideration of them cannot be carried to the extent of relieving the enemy of the penalties he has occurred. Lord Palmerston once wrote to a British ambassador in regard to an equally delicate matter: 'Tell them with all the politeness you are capable of that, whether they like it or not, nothing can prevent or alter the action of the British government.'

Our decision is taken, it has been forced upon us. No other course is open and no other will be taken.

If it be true that Germany, on seeing that another of her schemes has miscarried, offers to spare the lives of mariners and to cease her piracy if we withdraw our embargo on food, our answer is that the enemy has committed a crime and we can make no bargains with murderers and barbarians. America's jurisprudence does not provide for the acquittal of one who, having stabbed and robbed a man, promises not to use his knife upon his next victim.

Unloading horses from a ship at Gallipoli in 1915. Horses played a vital role in the war effort, especially in conflicts such as the Gallipoli Campaign. The campaign was fought to secure a sea route to Russia with the British and French launching a naval defensive forcing a passage through the Dardanelles. The ensuing land battle failed with the loss of many lives, including many Australians and New Zealanders.

On 2 March, the ship carrying the Plymouth Battalion was ordered once more to Gallipoli but again the landing was cancelled due to bad weather.

On 4 March at 8.30 am, the Plymouth Battalion landed companies at Sedd-el-Bahr and Kum Kale in order to destroy Turkish guns. The operation was successful but twenty-two men died and twenty-two were wounded.

On 3 March, Privates Charles Godfrey and David Ray of C Company 4th Battalion Highland Light Infantry, Plymouth, appeared in court in Exeter and were charged with being absent from their regiment, without leave, since 1 March. Evidence was given by PC Skinner, who stated that the defendants had asked him to show them the way back to the Town Barracks. They wanted a warrant to get back. In court, Inspector Sandford stated that an escort was being sent from Plymouth to take them back. They were remanded in custody and the PC received a reward of five shillings.

On 4 March, the steam collier *Thordis* arrived at Plymouth. Her master, Captain Bell, claimed that the vessel had successfully sunk a German submarine. This was later confirmed by the Admiralty. This entitled him to a prize of £1,160, which had been offered by *Syren and Shipping* and a Mr Crowpe, who was a reader of the *Yorkshire Post*.

The editor of *Syren and Shipping* received a telegram from Captain Bell that read:

> *The Thordis has been dry docked and one blade of her propeller is gone and a keel plate badly damaged. The Admiralty is satisfied that the submarine was sunk.*

When the *Thordis* arrived at Plymouth on Tuesday night, the captain reported that they had indeed rammed a German submarine. His log entry read:

> *At sea, Feb 28 – About 9.30 in the morning, while proceeding from Blyth toward Plymouth and Beachy Head, bearing northeast by north a distance of eight to ten miles, I observed the periscope of a submarine on the starboard bow. Ordered all hands on deck in case of emergency. Then observed a submarine*

The steam collier Thordis *arrived at Plymouth on 4 March 1915. Her master, Captain Bell, claimed that the vessel had successfully sunk a German submarine. This was later confirmed by the Admiralty and entitled him to a prize of £1,160.*

pass across our bow on to the port beam, where it took up a position thirty to forty yards off. Shortly afterward, I noticed the wake of a torpedo on the starboard beam. Put the helm hard over to starboard and ran over the periscope, when I and the crew heard and felt the crash under the bottom of our ship. Did not see the submarine after that but saw oil floating on the water. Proceeded on voyage.

On 25 March, the 3/4th, 3/5th and 3/6th Battalions of the Devonshire Regiment were formed at Exeter, Plymouth and Barnstaple before being moved to Barnstable in August.

On 26 March, it was reported that sixty-four wounded German prisoners had arrived at Devonport from Southampton and were conveyed to the fortress hospital.

On 28 March, Robert Laird, a private in the Highland Light Infantry was committed for trial by the Plymouth magistrates accused of the manslaughter of David Welsh, a private in the same regiment, at Fort Rennie near Plymouth.

Laird was demonstrating with a rifle in the barracks when a bullet was discharged from the weapon. The bullet passed through a door and killed Welsh instantly. Evidence said that the men were the best of friends and that dummy cartridges were normally used. However, a live cartridge was found to be missing.

On 19 April, a court in Newton Abbot heard a tale from a man claiming to be a deserter. The story read:

I had a glass or two of beer to drown my sorrows' was the excuse advanced by John Smith, 'a traveller', who, together with his wife, Ellen Smith, was charged with being drunk and disorderly at Newton Abbot on Saturday night.

'You ought to be ashamed – making beasts of yourself in war time,' remarked the Chairman, Dr J W Ley, who, with Mr A J Murrin CC, tried the case at Newton Abbot Police Court yesterday. Prisoners were stated to belong to Plymouth.

PC Butt stated that about 10 o'clock, the male defendant came to the police station and said he wished to give himself up as a deserter. Asked to leave, he became abusive and had to be forced out. Then he went down the street using disgusting language and was arrested.

Prisoner was now anxious to disclaim having been in the Army. 'Never been a soldier in my life,' he declared. 'I only wanted to get in for the night. We could not get lodgings anywhere and didn't want to be about the streets. I begged and prayed for lodgings but could not get any.'

'He had money enough to get lodgings,' said Inspector Browne, 'and if he had asked for them in a proper manner, he could have got them.'

In reference to the charge against the female defendant, PC Kellaway gave evidence of finding her leaning against a wall, drunk in East Street. She became very disorderly and abusive and a crowd collected.

Inspector Browne said prisoners were previously warned the same evening. They appeared to get their living by making imitation roses out of turnips.

Prisoners both professed sorrow and said they would clear out of the town at once.

> *Inspector Browne said it would not be fair for the people of the town to let them come there and make a disturbance, get board and lodging for a couple of nights, and then go away to another town and then do the same.*
>
> *'We will turn over a new leaf, sir,' said the male defendant.*
>
> *Fined 6s each or seven days. Prisoners asked for time to pay.*
>
> *'You will have to find the money or go to prison,' replied the Chairman. 'You ought to have thought about that before you made beasts of yourselves.'*

The *Sydney Mail* of 21 April, 1915 reported:

> *A German submarine stopped the French steamer Frederick Franck (973 tons). The commander demanded money, which was refused. He then tore up the French flag and threw the ship's papers into the sea. The Germans then exploded two bombs before the crew was able to leave, but these did not sink the vessel, which was towed to Plymouth.*
>
> *The German submarine, U24 caught the Glasgow steamer President, near Eddystone Lighthouse, after an hour's chase. The crew took to the boats. The U24's crew boarded the President and placed a bomb aboard. The vessel was still afloat when last seen. The submarine towed the crew to a fishing smack nearby.*

In May, the 3rd Battalion of the Devonshire Regiment set up headquarters in Plymouth, stationing themselves at Mount Wise, Granby and Raglan Barracks. They were a training unit used as part of the defences of Plymouth and remained in the UK throughout the war.

On 6 May, the *Cornishman* carried the news of the funeral of a Chief Petty Officer in Plymouth. The report read:

> *On Wednesday morning, the remains of Chief Petty Officer James Curnow, RN, who died at the Royal Albert Hospital, Devonport, on Friday night from injuries received through being knocked down by a tram car the same evening, were removed by rail to Marazion, for interment at Towednack.*

After the inquest on Saturday, the body was conveyed to the RN Hospital, Stonehouse and its removal to Millbay Station on Wednesday was carried out with naval honours, so highly was the deceased respected by his shipmates. Petty-officers acted as pall bearers and several chief petty officers walked behind the gun carriage. The ship's band attended and played Beethoven's and Chopin's funeral marches en route while a large funeral party, under Lieutenant Bradford, brought up the rear of the procession.

Wreaths were sent by the chief petty officers, Royal Marines, 'His Topmates', artificer staff, stokers and seamen.

On 28 May, the trial of Stoker PO Frederick Frost took place at a naval court-martial at Devonport. Frost, of *HMS Vivid*, was charged with allowing his patrol to accept drinks while on duty. He was also charged with failing to arrest a bluejacket in the street out of bounds. The charges were not proven and the accused was aquitted.

Plymouth Argyle finished in 17th place at the end of the 1914-1915 season. Their place was just four from the bottom although most clubs were unconcerned by their position with the more grim news filling the newspapers.

Lieutenant Corporal William Lockwood Lang of the 30th Corp. Regiment Engineers, motor cycle section, at Mount Wise Barracks, Plymouth.

Alfred Gard, a director of Argyle, and Bob Jack took charge of the club at the end of the season and no further competitive matches took place over the next four years. There were, however, the occasional games involving Armed Services' teams.

Moses Russell enlisted in the army and served in the Army Service Corps as a private in the mechanised transport section. He was later awarded the British War Medal and the Victory Medal.

The Royal Albert Hospital, Devonport. Part of the hospital was taken over by the Admiralty in the First World War and served as a War College and Port Library. In 1918 electric lighting was fitted with funds raised by the nursing staff.

In June 1915, Ford School was taken over by the military authorities.

On 10 June, the 28th (Northwest) Battalion, from Winnipeg, Canada, arrived at Plymouth before being stationed at Dibgate Camp near Folkstone. This formed part of the second contingent from Canada, which was under the command of Lieutenant-Colonel J. F. L. Embury of Regina.

The Royal Engineers carried out alterations on Hyde Park School so that the building could open as a hospital on 13 June. It included an extra 223 beds as well as twenty-two beds in tents. Wounded Australians who had returned from the Battle of Gallipoli occupied 185 of the beds.

In July, Ford Workhouse was also converted into a hospital with 435 beds and became the headquarters of the 4th Southern General Hospital.

On 3 July, the British steamship *Craigard* was sunk by a torpedo fired from a German submarine. The crew later landed safely at

Plymouth. The *Craigard* had set sail from Galveston on 3 June en route to Havre.

On 16 July, it was reported that cruelty to nationals by the allies breached international law. A Red Book issued by the Austro-Hungarian Ministry of Foreign Affairs told of all kinds of horrors and atrocities mostly against Austrians and Germans. Most of the offences took place overseas but also mentioned was Great Britain:

> *In Great Britain, insufficient food and accommodations, it is claimed, were accorded the interned nationals at Devonport and Newbury. Colonel Haines (presumably in charge of the detention camps) says that in a letter from Baron Giskra to Count Berchtold, 'he would have been quite willing to do something for the prisoners but his humanitarian impulses were checked by Lord Kitchener.*

Similar complaints were made by prisoners at Dorchester and at the concentration camp at Douglas on the Isle of Man.

On 8 September, it was announced that C. J. Maish, a wireless operator from New York, had been released from naval barracks in Plymouth. Maish had been the wireless operator on the Norwegian steamer *Seattle* and had been held in custody since the capture of the ship off the Falkland Islands on 14 March. Maish was released after representations made by the American Embassy. Another naturalised American citizen, George Vielmetter, who had been a steward on board the *Seattle,* was still being held at naval barracks in Plymouth. However, his release was expected shortly. The plight of the pair became known in July when details of their capture were brought to light by the American minister at Montevideo, Uruguay. The American Embassy informed the Foreign Office that the men had been on board the steamer *Bangor*, which had set sail from the Falklands. The embassy then received a report from the American consul in Plymouth that the two men were being held to give testimony at a prize court if the *Bangor*, which was now renamed the *Seattle*, later arrived at Plymouth.

The American consul at Dakar, Senegal, informed the embassy that the two men had gained his attention by waving their American passports at him from a porthole as he visited the Belgian steamer *Albertville*. The two men had been transferred to the *Albertville* when the *Bangor* arrived at Freetown, West Africa, from Port Stanley in the Falkland Islands. The ship had been held in the harbour at Port Stanley from 14 March until 19 July.

The British cruiser *Bristol* had previously captured the *Bangor*, which was charged with being engaged in unneutral service. At the time of capture, the *Bangor* had been transporting coal and provisions destined for the German auxiliary cruiser *Kronprinz Wilhelm*.

On 8 September, King George V and Queen Mary arrived in Plymouth on the Royal Train. They inspected the troops and awarded medals at Brickfields. They toured the seven military and naval hospitals in Plymouth before boarding the Royal Train at Devonport Station. Then they travelled on to Horrabridge, where they stayed the night.

On 9 September, King George V and Queen Mary travelled back to Plymouth, arriving at North Road Station. They continued their visits to local hospitals and afterwards visited Devonport Dockyard where they again awarded medals. In the evening, they once more travelled

The king reviewing troops at Devonport on 8 September 1915. The king, together with Queen Mary, arrived in Plymouth on the Royal Train. They inspected the troops and awarded medals at Brickfields before touring the seven military and naval hospitals in Plymouth.

King George V became king on 6 May 1910. The German Kaiser, Wilhelm II, was the king's first cousin. Many of the royal family had German titles due to their descent. George changed the name of the British royal house on 17 July 1917 from the House of Saxe-Coburg and Gotha to the House of Windsor. The former name was felt to be too German sounding for the British public. Both he and his relatives relinquished all their German titles soon after.

to Horrabridge before continuing their journey onwards to Exeter, where they paid a surprise visit.

On 17 September, it was reported that children of Ivy House Council School, Broadwoodwidger, had collected 3,312 eggs for wounded soldiers and sailors, which was an average of 114 per week over the preceding twenty-nine weeks. Two of the children, Miss Olive Shopland and Master Cyril Matthews, wrote their names and addresses on the eggs they sent and received many letters thanking them. One came from a wounded soldier in Plymouth and read:

12046 Gunner E Billings, 1st Seige Battery, RGA, A2 War, 4th Southern General Hospital, Plymouth, Wednesday Sept. 1st, 1915.
Dear Miss Olive,

When I was served out with my eggs today, I received one with your name and address written on it, so I must write and thank you for your kind thoughtfulness in thinking of us chaps. You may be sure we appreciate your kindness and it cheers us up to know that the little people of our dear old country think of us as well. You must be a nice little girl for nine years of age and you write very nicely too. I am in here suffering from wounds which I got at that awful place called Ypres. I got shot right through my thigh and the abdomen and nearly died. I am getting quite well again but shall never walk properly any more. I am much taller than you, being 6ft high, so you can guess how I feel it. But you know the song the soldiers sing, 'We are not downhearted yet,' so I am not going to be downhearted either. What do you think about it? I hope you and all your brothers and sisters, if you have any, are quite well, and your Pa and Ma also. Think I will close now as I am lying down writing this. So goodbye and good luck and best wishes from yours sincerely, E Billings.

Another letter read:

19781 Private J Bell, 3rd East Lanc., Ward E3, Salisbury Road Hospital, Plymouth, Wednesday, Sept. 1st, 1915.

Dear Friend,

I am writing a few lines to you although I am a stranger to you, but I thank you very much for the egg which I received this morning with your address written on it. I thought that you would like to know where it had got to; so now you will know. I hope you don't mind me writing these few lines to you, as I am only a soldier who is doing his bit for his King and country until I was admitted in hospital for appendicitis. I am now getting on very well, although I have been in for nearly a month, and I am still in bed yet but I am hoping to get up before very long. I am sorry to say that I don't know where Lifton is, but there is one thing I know, and that is your address. I hope you are in the best of health and you will continue to be so for the rest of your life. I will now close my letter to you and I am hoping to hear from you again before very long. I remain, yours truly, Pte. Bell.

The *Cornishman* of 7 October, reported that the miltary hospital at Salisbury Road had burned down but said that all 'inmates' were saved. The fire had taken hold on the morning of 5 October. The end block of the building was found on fire at 3 am. Luckily that area of the hospital was empty as it was undergoing repair work at the time and this allowed everyone to escape safely.

On 9 October, the *Western Times* carried the following story of the arrest of a burglar:

Not Fit to Fight by Side of Decent Men.
At the Plymouth Quarter Sessions yesterday, before the recorder, Mr J A Hawke K C, Joseph Taylor, a soldier, pleaded guilty to a charge of burglary.

PS Mollart, of West Bromwich, proved a previous conviction at the Quarter Sessions there in May 1914 for felony. Prisoner, he stated, was released from prison on February 13th, 1914, on license, and reported himself at Porth, in Glamorgan, where a situation was found for him. He made his way to Staffordshire and in May was sentenced to six months for felony at West Bromwich. He next reappeared at his home in khaki. He was given lodgings but the following morning, it was found that he had disappeared and goods and money to the value of £7 were missing.

Answering the Recorder, the prisoner said that he knew there was a charge of felony against him at Tipton. He pleaded guilty to it and wished it to be dealt with in conjunction with the present charge.

PS Mollart said everything possible had been done for the prisoner at different times when he had been liberated from prison. He had spent five years in a reformatory and there was a conviction against him as far back as 1889.

Prisoner said that he came out of Dartmoor with only two shillings between him and the gutter. What could they expect a man in that position to do? Prisoner expressed his sorrow. He was returning to camp at the time and was under the influence of drink. He added that he had been hoping to go to the front and hoped that he would be given a chance.

Addressing prisoner, the Recorder said that it was difficult for him to find any reason why he should treat him mercifully.

Canadian troops in the trenches. The troops are shown here fixing bayonets, ready for any future hand-to-hand fighting. The troops were said to have shown remarkable bravery and were steadfast in defence.

So far as his record showed, his age must be more than he said it was, for the 26 years that he had been in and out of prison. He (the Recorder) gathered that some months ago he did the right thing and joined the Army, and if since he had behaved himself and taken the chance given him, he would have been able to treat him mercifully. But since he had been in the Army, this was not the only offence that he had committed.

'As for being sent to the front,' added the Recorder, 'so far as I have anything to show, I don't think it would be my duty to send you to fight by the side of decent men. That is the trouble.'

Prisoner was sent to gaol for twelve months.

As the war progressed, Plymouth's local newspaper, the *Evening Herald*, replaced many of the usual adverts found on its front page with 'War' and 'Foreign' news. The news told of the appalling death rate at the front.

A report in the *Evening Herald* of 14 October 1915 read:

Officers of the 3/5th Battalion, Devon Regiment, made practical use of Tavistock Goose Fair yesterday. They saw crowds of young fellows in 'civilians' about – almost as many of them as their khaki-clad brothers. A motor-car arranged with recruiting posters was driven about the streets, and the RAMC band paraded, playing popular airs. The numbers who joined up as a result were fourteen – all well-built young fellows.

In October, Camel's Head School was also requisitioned by military authorities.

On 16 November, the *Western Times* reported that under the Defence of the Realm Act (Liquor Control), from 22 November public houses in and around Plymouth would only be allowed to open between 12 noon and 2.30 pm and 6 pm to 9 pm on weekdays. On Sundays, public houses couldn't open until 2.30 pm. The paper stated that under the order 'no treating is allowed'.

On 23 November, two captured German machine-guns were drawn in procession through the streets of Plymouth with a view to encouraging men to recruit. There was much enthusiasm as the guns passed by. The Mayor of Plymouth, Mr T. Baker, expressed the wish that the town would one day have a permanent display of captured German guns.

In December, *Little Red Riding Hood* was announced as this year's pantomime at the Theatre Royal in Plymouth.

On 22 December, the public were notified that the maximum weight of parcels that could be sent to the military forwarding office at Devonport was 56 pounds. Arrangements were made with the railway companies to refuse any parcel that was heavier. It was requested that clothes, food and tobacco intended for British subjects interned at Ruhleben be in future sent to the United States Ambassador in Berlin or to Mr Powell, captain of the camp. The dispatch of any goods in bulk to other persons was prohibited.

Meals in the trenches usually consisted of bully beef but behind the lines the food could be quite varied as shown here on Christmas Day 1915. A tray of plump chickens has been prepared for the men as they are called to the cookhouse by a bugler of the Army Veterinary Corps.

A soldier receives letters and parcels from home. Troops were much cheered by parcels of gifts from home, which contained cakes 'that mother made', hand-knitted socks, which were said to be much better than the army issue ones, and 'fags', which were much prized.

On 27 December, the *Western Times* reported a fatality in Plymouth. The story read:

Yesterday, while a number of motor vehicles were proceeding through Plymouth, one skidded and collided with a cab, which was swung into a shop window. A sixteen months' old child of Mrs Edith Williams was killed. Several other people were injured.

On 28 December, a report stated that 800 wounded soldiers from the Serbian campaign had arrived safely in Plymouth after travelling from the Mediterranean.

A report in the *Evening Herald* of 28 December read:

Notes of the Day:
There were few or none of the memorable incidents of Christmas 1914 about Christmas 1915 in the trenches. Too many barbarities have happened in the year to allow the men to favour an unofficial truce, foremost, the villainy of the poison gas; but other memories, from the sinking of the Lusitania *to the execution of Nurse Cavell, have embittered the memories of the British soldiers. Their one desire is to beat the Germans.*

A report in the *Evening Herald* of 29 December stated:

The Cabinet held a critical, but decisive meeting yesterday. It is understood that the majority of Ministers agreed on the recruiting question, and to introduce a means of compulsion for unmarried men.

CHAPTER 3

1916
The Realisation

Compulsory enlistment for men between the ages of 18 and 41 was introduced for single men and childless widowers. However, essential war workers, clergymen, the physically unfit and approved conscientious objectors were exempt. The upper age was later raised to 51.

On 13 January, the *Cornishman* reported that the pantomime *Little Red Riding Hood* was still going strong at the Theatre Royal with crowded houses nightly. Matinees were said to be packed with children who were accompanied by their 'sisters, cousins, aunts and even uncles'. The show was described as 'the best pantomime seen in the West Country for many years'.

On 15 January, the British South African liner *Appam*, en route for Plymouth, was captured by Germans off the Canary Islands. There were 451 people on board, including 138 survivors from seven other ships sunk by the same German raider.

Phyllis Sehllcht, from Torquay, appeared before the Plymouth magistrates on Friday 21 January. Her husband was described as a German waiter. She was charged, as an

A recruitment poster stating 'Women of Britain say Go!' In January 1916, the Military Service Bill was introduced forcing the conscription of single men between the ages of 18 and 41. In May, conscription was extended to married men also.

Pupils at Morice Town School in 1916. Apart from everyday subjects, lessons also included the latest updates on the war including any victories or defeats. Many children in class would have fathers fighting away in the war and eagerly awaited news.

alien ememy, with unlawfully entering a prohibited area without obtaining a permit. She was also charged with being an alien residing in Plymouth and failing to provide to the registration officer the necessary documents. She pleaded guilty and was fined ten shillings for each offence.

On 22 January, Plymouth became the first town to be visited by Clara Butt as she began her annual tour in the west of the country. She was greeted by a huge audience. The *Cornishman* reported that the concert took place during 'uncomfortable conditions of weather'. It was reported that the audience arrived 'blown about and damp', but any discomfort was soon forgotten as the concert got underway. Accompaniment was provided by the Plymouth Orpheus Male Choir conducted by a Mr Parkes. Clara Butt and the choir performed *Land of Hope and Glory*, which was greatly received. The tour continued through Cornwall to Penzance calling at Truro and Falmouth on the way.

The *Evening Post* of 1 February reported:

ANZAC HEROES DEPART.
The second contingent of New Zealand soldiers, unfit for further

Clara Butt with her husband Kennerley Rumford. Clara Butt visited Plymouth on 22 January 1916. She was famous for being a recitalist and concert singer and sang for many service charities during the First World War.

military service, left Plymouth last week by the Rotorna. The men had a great reception from the Devon folk. The Band of the Royal Garrison Artillery played the ship away from the harbour and there was much cheering. Major Brereton was in charge of the New Zealanders on board.

An Admiralty Order was published in the *London Gazette* on 1 February stating that under the Defence of the Realm Regulations, pilot licences should be suspended, where Trinity House seems fit, of all present pilots as well as the suspension of certificates of all masters and mates from Plymouth eastwards towards Great Yarmouth. No licence was to be granted for longer than fourteen days.

In February, there were fears of a Zeppelin attack when one drifted slowly across Plymouth. In nearby Exeter, and many other towns and cities, streets were darkened because of the worry of similar German raids.

On 10 February, seventy-two survivors of the Japanese steamship *Takata Maru* were landed at Plymouth. They were rescued by the American steamer *Silver Shell*, with which she collided on 2 February whilst 200 miles south-east of Cape Race.

On 6 March, a member of the Plymouth Brethren was refused exemption from war service at the Kirkcaldy Military Tribunal. The

A Zeppelin in flight watched by many onlookers. The German High Command thought that Zeppelins were the ideal way to carry out bombing raids on England. However, they soon realised their vulnerability after several were shot down by British airmen, landing in a ball of flames.

applicant, who was a Methil watchmaker, stated that no one belonging to the Plymouth Brethren should take part in warfare. Also at the tribunal were four members of the Royal Scots, who had applied for exemption due to financial hardship. Their request was refused. A pianist at Kirkcaldy Picture House applied for exemption on conscientious grounds. His application was refused. Twenty-two applicants were granted temporary exemption and seven claims were refused. Two conditional and three contingency exemptions were granted.

Showing at the Theatre Royal in Plymouth, commencing 13 March, was *The Passing Show*, which was one of the biggest productions to be staged in Plymouth.

By March, many newspapers carried reports

An enlistment poster stating 'The Empire Needs Men!' Propaganda posters issued by the government urged men to enlist. Many were exempt due to their jobs, such as essential workers employed within the dockyard. Many men claimed exemption because they worked on farms. Some appealed as Conscientous Objectors citing religious or moral reasons.

of tribunals of men claiming exemption from the army due to conscientous, religious, work or other reasons.

On 17 March, the *Western Times* carried the story of Robert Skerret who had applied for exemption due to conscientous grounds. Cross examining him a Mr Heath asked:

> *What is your objection to fighting?*
> *Applicant: It is not in accordance with the teachings of God that I should take up arms to kill my fellow man.*
> *Mr Heath: You do kill some things I suppose; rabbits, for instance?*
> *Applicant: No, Sir. I never get the chance.*
> *Mr Heath: I suppose there were wars in days of old. God instructed them to kill?*
> *Applicant: No. Not to my knowledge.*
> *Mr Heath: Do you read the Bible? What about Gideon, the Israelites and those people?*
> *Applicant: I don't know.*
> *Mr Heath: What do you belong to?*
> *Applicant: The Plymouth Brethren.*
> *The chairman: Do you keep pigs?*
> *Applicant: Yes.*
> *The chairman: Do you have them killed?*
> *Applicant: Yes, sir.*
> *The chairman: You don't mind their being killed?*
> *Applicant: That's different. That was ordained for food.*
> *The chairman: The pig would not look at it from that point of view.*
> *(laughter)*

The case was postponed to 14 May.

On 18 March, newspaper reports carried the story of the death of a young cadet. The story read:

> *An inquest was opened at the Royal Naval Hospital, Plymouth yesterday respecting the death of Cadet Donald Addenbrooke.*
> *The Coroner stated that the deceased was boxing with another cadet at the Royal Naval College in Devonport when he*

received a blow and fell to the floor. It was then noticed that he had received the injury to his skull. He was admitted to hospital on Monday last, and died yesterday morning.

No evidence was called and the inquest was adjourned till Monday next. Deceased was a native of Edinburgh.

On 22 March, newspapers reported that Vice-Admiral Sir J. S. Warrender had assumed command of the naval station at Plymouth. He succeeded Admiral Sir George Le Clerc Egerton, who had held the post since March 1913.

On Friday 23 March, Dorace Grace Briggs, aged 19, appeared before the Plymouth Justices charged, while working for the postmaster general, with stealing a letter containing a postal order and a payment card totalling 11 shillings and 4d. She had previously worked for the recruiting authorities within Plymouth having originally come from Bristol.

She was defended by Mr Isaac Foot, who said that she had come from a good home and her previous character wasn't called into disrepute. Dr Watson Williams said that the defendant suffered from a nasal/ear problem, which had affected her judgement, stating that the patient often lived in a dreamy state. The doctor stated that he had known of several similar cases. The accused was bound over for six months and placed in the care of her aunt, who had travelled from Bristol to attend the case.

On 31 March, it was reported that the price of wheat had dropped by a shilling at Driffield, Yorkshire and Plymouth.

An inquest on 6 April, passed a verdict of 'found dead' on a telegraphist at the Plymouth Post Office. Miss Gertrule Chellew's body was found mutilated at a level crossing at Yelverton.

On the same day a memorial was held for Reverend F. W. Hewitt, who was killed at the Battle of Loos while acting as forces chaplain. The memorial was dedicated at Brixton Church near Plymouth.

On 12 April, the inquest into the death of a soldier at Crownhill Fort took place. Private L. Walker, aged 36, of Fishponds, Bristol had served at the fort for about a week. Private C. Arberry stated that at 9 am the company had marched to the fort to get tools. Once on the parade ground, Walker dropped down dead. The coroner stated that the cause of death was due to 'a rupture of the right ventricle of the heart which might have been caused by the marching'. He noted that there was *'a fatty degeneration to that organ'*. A verdict of natural causes was recorded.

The *North Devon Journal* of 13 April reported that two men had tried to jump on board a steamer as it was leaving Pottery Quay in Devonport. One was successful but the other man fell into the water and drowned. Several lifebuoys had been thrown to him but to no avail.

On 14 April, newspapers carried the story of the death of a Mrs Moore of Torrington Place, Plymouth who was 105 years old when she died.

On 23 April, Major-General Dobell and Brigadier Cunliffe arrived at Plymouth after the completion of the Cameroons campaign.

On 27 April, Hubert Wilkes was summoned to the police court in Dover for the non-attendance of his two sons at school. The court heard that Wilkes was a soldier serving at Plymouth and the case was dismissed so that the mother could be summoned.

Canadian troops eating their midday meal in a well-sandbagged trench. The men are wearing steel helmets that were worn by Canadian troops in action for the first time during April 1916.

Your

Thankoffering

for

VICTORY

Buy National War Bonds. It is your duty, your privilege, your best thank-offering to the men who have fought and won

An advert for National War Bonds. An advert that appeared in April 1916 urged people to purchase War Bonds. It read: 'Lend your money to your country. The soldier does not grudge offering his life to his country. He offers it freely, for his life may be the price of Victory. But Victory cannot be won without money as well as men, and your money is needed. Unlike the soldier, the investor runs no risk. If you invest in Exchequer Bonds your money, capital and interest alike, is secured on the Consolidated Fund of the United Kingdom, the premier security of the world.'

On 1 May, Great Western Railway's ambulance trains were exhibited at Millbay Docks. They included sixteen coaches with room for 592 men. They were manned by forty-five medical staff. An official visit to the trains was paid on 2 May by the Mayor and Deputy Mayor of Plymouth, Aldermen T. Baker and E. Blackall.

On 1 May, a tramway fatality was reported in the *Western Times*. The article stated:

A street collision in Plymouth in which a runaway motor lorry ran into a tramway car, causing the latter to travel backwards down a steep hill, resulted in the death from a skull fracture of a woman named as Elizabeth Gilly. At the inquest, a verdict of 'Accidental death' was recorded.

On 6 May, the body of Major H. A. Carter arrived in Plymouth from East Africa. He had been killed in January, two days after he arrived in East Africa after travelling with his regiment from France. Previously, thirteen years before, he had won the Victoria Cross in Somaliland.

On 20 May, the prime minister of Australia, William Hughes, arrived at Devonport with his wife and Andrew Fisher, the high

William Morris 'Billy' Hughes was an Australian politician who was the seventh Australian prime minister between 1915 and 1923. Hughes supported Australia's participation in the First World War. After 28,000 Australians were either killed, wounded or missing during July and August 1916, Generals Birdwood and White of the Australian Imperial Force suggested to Hughes that conscription was the only way to continue the country's participation in the war effort.

commissioner for Australia. They were the guests of the commander-in-chief at Admiralty House. The following day, they visited the dockyard before journeying on to London.

On 22 May, the D. W. Griffith play *Birth of a Nation* was performed at the Theatre Royal in Plymouth. It had been a huge success in both London and New York. The spectacular show featured scenes from America's Civil War as well as scenes showing the Ku Klux Clan. The show was described as 'a gigantic production which involved great preparation'.

A report in the *Evening Herald* of 3 June read:

> *The Plymouth historian, R A J Walling concluded of the Battle of Jutland that: "No single battle in history has inflicted such loss and suffering on Plymouth."*

On 16 June, the *Western Times* reported several cases of applications for exemption from active service. Some were due to agriculture reasons. The article read:

The smiling faces of sailors returning from the Battle of Jutland. The number of sailors injured at Jutland included fifty-one officers and 513 men.

At the sitting of the Devon Appeal Tribunal at Plymouth on Monday, an appeal against the refusal to give further time was made on behalf of Nicholas P Luscombe, farmer and market gardener, Brixham, a single unattested man. The Board of Agricultural representative suggested exemption until the harvest was got in. Exemption until August was allowed.

There were two appeals against the exemption granted to George Vanstone, cowman, Tavistock, employed by Mr Lillicrap, farmer and wholesale cattle dealer. One was lodged by Mr WR Fox, local military representative, and the other by Major Strode, recruiting officer. Mr Fox, giving evidence, said the employer had let a great portion of his farm. This case had hindered recruiting in the neighbourhood. Vanstone was single and age 32.

Clerk: 'If this man is a cowman and 32, he is in a certified occupation.'

Mr Fox: 'He is not a cowman, he is a drover.'

Mr Lillicrap said that Vanstone was an excellent cowman and his only employee except for a decrepit old man. He (Mr Lillicrap) dealt with from 2,000 to 3,000 bullocks and about 5,000 sheep every year. Vanstone's wages were about £2 a week

(30s and extras). The case was adjourned for two months to enable the employer to find a substitute.

Conditional exemption for three months was given to Walter Abbott, working foreman, employed by Mr Sampson, Buckfastleigh, the condition being that he remains in his present class of employment. Abbott was 27 and a married man.

The appeal of Alfred Bate, wholesale and retail grocer of 95 High Street, Totnes, on behalf of WJ le Duc, his assistant, was disallowed. The local tribunal considered that the staff would be sufficient if le Duc joined the army. Appellant said he could not carry on his business with less male labour than he had at present.

Jasper John Callard, farmer, Buckfastleigh, had been granted conditional exemption until December 1st, on undertaking to drill regularly, but the military appealed. Callard said in addition to his land, he had a grist mill. The ground of appeal was that Callard was disposing of much of his stock. Decision of local tribunal upheld.

The father of James Millman, 34, single man, Buckfastleigh, appealed unsuccessfully on behalf of his son, who managed his motor garages.

The appeal of Lieutenant-Colonel Downing DSO, Totnes on behalf of William Howard, his groom-gardener and caretaker, who had been given four weeks' exemption by the local tribunal, was dismissed. Colonel Downing, who was on sick leave from the front, attended to support the appeal.

Several other cases were also heard at the tribunal.

On 18 June, a Mr John Elliott of Admiral's Hard, Stonehouse, received a postcard from his son, Frederick, stating that he was now a prisoner-of-war in Germany. He was captured during a naval battle while serving on the *Indefatigable*.

On Monday 19 June, the body of Alice Clara Gregory, aged 12, was found in a field near to Plymouth. A Private in the Worcester Regiment later confessed to her murder. Frederick Brooks, alias Jones, aged 28, had earlier surrendered to police.

The *Western Times* of 19 June reported that the Devon and Cornwall Branch of the National Poor Law Officers Association was held at the

Women look for news of their men. Wives and mothers eagerly scanned any notices posted containing lists of casualties. A crowd would gather when any new news was issued. Daily columns of deceased and wounded servicemen also appeared in local newspapers.

Exeter City Workhouse presided over by Mr E. Birch of Devonport. He said that it wasn't just sufficient to relieve poverty but to find the cause of it. He spoke of the hardship felt by soldiers and their families. The paper reported:

> *Even this week, he had heard of a case in Plymouth where a soldier had returned from the front wounded, had been discharged from hospital recovered, but had been discharged from the Army as unfit for further service and was in great need for himself, his wife and children.*

He went on to say:

There will be thousands of such cases when the war is over and it is for the officers entrusted with the duties of relieving the poor and needy to speedily consider this subject and formulate some scheme which would be of a national service and a blessing to mankind.

On 27 June, Frederick Brooks appeared before the Plymouth Police Court charged with the murder of Clara Gregory, whose body had been found in a field at Lower Compton. Her parents lived nearby in Alexander Road. At a subsequent inquest a verdict of 'wilful murder' was returned against the prisoner, who had earlier given himself up and had helped police search for the body. The evidence given said that the soldier had previously called at the girl's school to pick her up after becoming acquainted with the girl's relatives. Calling himself Mr Jones, he told the headmistress that her parents had sent him with a message to collect the girl from school so that she could help him find a place with which he wasn't acquainted. She was allowed to leave the school but was later found strangled. Brooks was committed for trial at the next Assizes at Exeter.

The 13th (Works) Battalion were formed in Saltash in June before moving to Plymouth. They would later become the 3rd Labour Battalion in April 1917.

As the Battle of the Somme raged in Europe, relatives back in Plymouth dreaded a knock on the door, as they had throughout the war, of the telegram boy bringing news of their loved ones' deaths. Newspapers carried the news of all wounded and killed soldiers.

The death-columns of the *Herald* provide a pointer to the extent of the tragedies of Jutland and of the first battle of the Somme. An eye-witness reported:

We passed along the line of German ships some miles away. The air was heavy with masses of smoke black, yellow, green, of every colour, which drifted between the opposing lines. Again and again salvoes of shells fell short of the mark. I watched the Iron Duke *swinging through the seas, letting off broadside after broadside, wicked tongues of flames leaping through clouds of smoke. The din of battle was stunning, stupendous, deafening, as hundreds of the heaviest guns in the world gave tongue at once. All [officers] on board the* Indefatigable, *the* Defence *and the* Black Prince *were lost; only four of the* Queen Mary *and two of the* Invincible *were saved. The list of officers killed numbers 333, and included Rear Admirals Hood, and Arbuthnot, whose flags were carried on the* Invincible *and* Defence *respectively.*

On 9 July, Admiral Sir George Warrender gave an address at the Plymouth Brotherhood. While there, he signed the petition for prohibition of drink during the war and six months afterwards.

The *Dundee Courier* of 12 July reported the story of a British airship sighted over Plymouth. The report read:

The people of Plymouth were greatly interested yesterday in the graceful spectacle of a British airship manoeuvring over the town. It flew at a low altitude and was clearly visible from all parts of the district.

One humorous incident in connection with the visit occurred at a Police Court sitting in a village in the vicinity. The Court was at once adjourned to enable all to witness the spectacle, leaving the prisoner alone in the dock.

A report on 14 July announced that wheat prices had risen in both Plymouth and Driffield.

On 18 July, James Stocks, who was a regular minister of the Plymouth Brethren, was brought before magistrates at the Petty Sessions at Bishops Lydeard in West Somerset. Stocks, aged 35, was charged with being an absentee from His Majesty's forces under the Military Service Act. Stocks claimed he was exempt from war service as he was a minister of the Plymouth Brethren. Mr C.P. Clarke who had prosecuted Stocks on behalf of the War Office stated that now his position within the church had been noted. It was decided not to press the prosecution.

On 18 July, HMAT (His Majesty's Australian Transport) Warilda *arrived in Plymouth from Fremantle, Western Australia, carrying Tunnelling Company 6, 3rd Tunnelling Company. The journey had taken over six weeks.*

On 21 July, in the column of deaths in the Western Times, it was reported that the well-known Plymouth boxer Sergeant Tom McCormick had been killed in action.

On 8 August, James 'Jimmy' McCormick, who played for Argyle 268 times up until 1915, was captured by the Germans during the Battle of the Somme. As a sergeant in 17th Middlesex (1st Footballers' Regiment), he was badly injured before being captured at Waterlot Farm, Guillemont. He was repatriated in November 1918 and continued to play for Argyle.

James 'Jimmy' McCormick played for Argyle 268 times up until 1915. He was captured while serving with the 17th Middlesex (1st Footballers' Regiment) during the Battle of the Somme on 8 August 1916.

Reports on 12 August mentioned details about the Shackleton relief ship:

The Antarctic relief ship Discovery *left Devonport on Thursday evening for Port Stanley, Falkland Islands, where she will take aboard Sir Ernest Shackleton and his party and make another attempt to rescue the 22 explorers marooned on Elephant Island, South Shetlands.*

The Discovery *has been fitted out at Devonport Dockyard and Lieutenant-Commander Fairweather is in charge.*

The 14th (Labour) Battalion was formed in Plymouth in August and, two months later, landed in France to join The Third Army.

During August, children and residents of Devonport witnessed wounded soldiers returning from the Battle of the Somme.

A report in the *Western Times* of 15 August stated that a Plymouth minister, the Reverend T. J. Chenalls said that people taking their children on

Sir Ernest Henry Shackleton led three expeditions to Antarctica. Between 1914 and 1917, Shackleton took part in the Imperial Trans-Antarctic Expedition. However, disaster struck when the expedition's ship, Endurance, *became trapped in ice before anyone could be landed. They eventually escaped with no loss of life and Shackleton returned to the Antarctic in 1921 as part of the Shackleton-Rowett Expedition.*

Wounded troops on board a train receive refreshments. Here the walking-wounded return to camp via a train with a stop on the way to receive a welcome drink. The more seriously wounded faced long tortuous journeys to crowded casualty centres before they were returned home.

Sunday outings to Whitsands or the country were involved in 'one of the most sinister and evil tendencies of our times'. The newly elected president of the Ebenezer Wesleyan Monthly Brotherhood received much applause when he gave his speech at the Guildhall. He went on the say, 'We must pray, not only for the end of the war, but for the conversion of Germany who have turned their back on the evangelical faith.' He went on to say that in a dug-out used by the Crown Prince of Germany there was found an altar-cloth from a nearby village church used as a carpet for the royal prince. He explained that the Germans' lack of faith and disregard for religious objects was responsible for much of their barbarity.

Newspapers on 28 August announced the wedding of the brother of Waldorf Astor, a Member of Parliament for Plymouth since 1911. Captain John J. Astor married Lady Nairne, who was the widow of Major Lord Charles Nairne who had been killed in the war. Astor was issued with a brief leave to allow him to marry by special licence at Christchurch before returning to France several hours later.

The *Poverty Bay Herald* of 28 August reported:

ANZAC MUNITION WORKERS ARRIVAL IN ENGLAND.
An interesting addition to the ranks of munition workers, says a
London paper, is a party of between 50 and 60 Australians who
have arrived in London. They left Melbourne on May 24th, bound
for Plymouth, and the party would have been larger had there
been more room on board. These men are no strangers to
England. Many took part at the landing at Gallipoli, and had been
in hospitals over here before being sent back to Australia. They
were all either fitters or turners, and though unfit for further active
service, they felt they could still assist by making munitions.

On 5 September, Co-op workers in Plymouth threatened strike action demanding an increase in wages.

On 14 September, the wedding of Lieutenant Herbert James took place at Stoke Damerel Church. Lieutenant Herbert had won a Victoria Cross in Gallipoli. His bride was Gladys Beatrice Lillicrap, the eldest daughter of Lieutenant F.W. Lillicrap of the Royal Engineers, formerly a water engineer to the Devonport Corporation.

On 12 October, the *Cornishman* newspaper reported that shipping was being held up at Plymouth because of an extension of the dockers' strike. The strike was in sympathy of workers at the Co-op.

On Saturday 14 October, the Co-op workers' strike still continued. several Labour leaders discussed, with the committee of the Plymouth Co-operative Society, a way to end the strike, but although the negotiations lasted several hours, nothing was resolved.

On 22 October 1916, Sergeant William James Baker was killed at Serre during the Battle of the Somme. Baker was a former professional footballer who played for Plymouth Argyle, and was a member of the 17th Battalion Middlesex Regiment (also known as the Footballers' Battalion). The Footballers' Battalion

William Baker played 202 games in the Southern League and FA
Cup for Plymouth Argyle between 1909 and 1915. He joined the
17th Battalion, Middlesex Regiment (the Footballers' Battalion)
but was killed in action on 22 October 1916, at Serre, during the
Battle of the Somme.

was made up of many talented footballers and Baker saw his first match as a player for the Green Waves (a local team) in 1901. After playing for the club for four seasons, he left to play in America and for De Beers in South Africa. He returned to Devon and once more played for the Green Waves before joining Plymouth Argyle in 1909. He made 200 appearances for the club, playing left-half for six seasons. He made his last appearance on 1 May 1915, playing away at Southend, before leaving for active service. He was described in the Argyle handbook as 'possessed of inexhaustible energy and indomitable pluck'. He was 33 years old when he died and was awarded the Military Medal. He is commemorated at the Sucrerie military cemetery at Colincamps.

The village of Serre was a stronghold of the Germans at the beginning of the Battle of the Somme. When the main attack took place on 1 July 1916, Serre was the most northern point, approximately 5 miles north of Albert. Many Pals battalions suffered heavy losses at Serre and were made up of colleagues, friends and relations.

Another player to die at the Battle of the Somme was Evelyn Lintott who played centre-half with Plymouth Argyle, Queen's Park Rangers, Bradford City and Leeds City. In his career he won seven full England caps. Lintott's full-time job was as a teacher and he continued to teach until he became a leading amateur. In the First World War, he served as a lieutenant in 15th Battalion, West Yorkshire Regiment (the Leeds Pals Regiment). He was killed by gunfire, aged 33, on 1st July. His body was never found although his name is recorded at the Thiepval Memorial together with 75,000 other men who lost their lives.

A letter to the *Yorkshire Post* stated:

Lieutenant Lintott's end was particularly gallant. Tragically, he was killed leading his platoon of the 15th West Yorkshire Regiment, The Leeds Pals, over the top. He led his men with great dash and when hit the first time declined to take the count. Instead, he drew his revolver and called for further effort. Again he was hit but struggled on but a third shot finally bowled him over.

Stanley Reed played for Argyle during the 1913-1914 season. He was also a very well-known Devon cricketer. In December 1915, he joined the 11th Devonshire Regiment as a lance-corporal. He died during training at Wareham in Dorset. On 21 April 1916, a grenade he was about to throw exploded in his left hand. He received severe head injuries and died almost instantly. He was just 21 years old.

Norman Wood played for Argyle twice before joining the Footballers' Battalion. He served as a sergeant and was killed on 28 July 1916 at Delville Wood during the Battle of the Somme.

As early as 22 October, H. Matthew and Sons of Bedford Street advertised for sale Christmas plum puddings. These could be shipped to the British Expeditionary Force, Egyptian Expeditionary Force, Salonika Force and the Mesopotamia Expeditionary Force for as little as 4/2 for a 2lb plum pudding.

Many men who had previously been found to be unfit for military service were now finding themselves passed as fit. One such case was reported in the *Western Times* of 24 October. It read:

Stanley Reed played for Argyle during the 1913-1914 season. He joined the 11th Devonshire Regiment as a Lance-Corporal in December 1915 and died during training at Wareham in Dorset on 21 April 1916.

> *Tavistock Urban Tribunal met Thursday, Mr J Backwell presiding. Mr H Chichester was the military representative.*
>
> *An interesting case was that of Percy J Gregory, single, 20, chauffeur and mechanic. It was stated that the applicant had served in the DCLI until November, 1914, when he was discharged as medically unfit. On going to Plymouth recently to be re-examined, he produced his discharge papers, which were taken from him and retained by the military authorities, whom afterwards placed him in C1. Several members of the tribunal expressed surprise at the conduct of the military in keeping the young man's discharge papers. The applicant was given until March 31st on the understanding that he joined the DVR.*

On 30 October, the *Andania*, belonging to the Cunard line, called at Plymouth to take on more coal for the forwarding journey to New York. There were fifty passengers on board who were on a twenty-three-day voyage from London. Newspapers reported that, while at sea, they had witnessed a battle in the English Channel and all had unanimously agreed that the war had taken the monotony out of ocean travel.

However, passengers arriving in Plymouth said they hadn't known

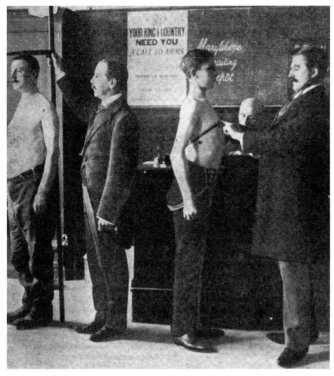

A youth and a man receiving a medical examination before being passed fit to enlist. In the background is a recruitment poster stating, 'Your King and country need you.'

that any military action had taken place in the Channel until they were informed at Plymouth that the British had lost eight trawlers, two destroyers and one transport. The Germans had lost two destroyers and one light cruiser.

On 6 November, the *Ausonia*, part of the Cunard Line, called at Plymouth to pick up passengers for the onward journey to Canada. Fares were £10 cabin rate and £6 10s for third class. The fares were advertised as being the cheapest prices anywhere on route to Canada.

On 6 December, hundreds of large packing cases containing Christmas presents for New Zealand troops arrived at Plymouth.

On 8 December, entertainment came from a heavyweight boxing match at the Plymouth Cosmopolitan Club. The two well-known heavyweights who took part were Bandsman Rice and Petty Officer Curran. The fight resulted in Rice winning the match on points.

When a deadlock was reached at the Western Front during Christmas 1916, it was possible, for the first time, to give the men Christmas leave. A spell at the Front, where spending was impossible, meant that the soldiers had acrued a nice balance of pay even though they only received 1s 1d a day. They were said to spend generously, many buying toy animals for their children back home.

On 12 December, the *Western Times* reported that the soldier Frederick Brooks, who had been found guilty of murdering 12-year-old Alice Clara Gregory on 19 June, would not be granted a reprieve from the death sentence handed to him by Mr Justice Rowlatt in November. The sentence was to be carried out at 8 am on 12 December and no press were allowed to attend, which had been the rule since 1885 with the failure to hang Babbacombe murderer John Lee.

The *Cornishman* of 14 December reported that:

'Messrs. Andrews' Picture Palaces show the finest war films and other films which reach the west of England.'

On 29 December, Thomas James Stayman, the captain of a steamer, aged 49, appeared before the Plymouth Police Court. Stayman, from North Shields, was charged with unlawfully and maliciously inflicting grievous bodily harm upon John Edward Jackson on the high seas on 30 November. He was further charged with the attempted murder of John Lloyd Jones Gifford on the high seas on 26 December. Mr S. Carlile Davis appeared for the prosecution and Mr Isaac Foot appeared for the defence. Detective-Inspector S. Lucas stated that signals were flown from a ship in the Sound requesting police help. Lucas and Detective-Sergeant Cloke boarded the ship and were taken to the captain's cabin which was barricaded and locked from the outside. When they removed the timber they found the captain handcuffed inside, who was described as looking 'vacant and very wild', and was under the influence of heavy drink.

In reply to the first charge, the captain stated, 'He struck me as much as I struck him.'

In reply to the second charge, he said, 'I deny it!'

He was refused bail and remanded in custody.

Also on 29 December, reports appeared in the *Evening Herald* that the Plymouth schooner *Constance Mary* had been sunk. The captain and crew were picked up by a Norwegian steamer, which took them back to port.

CHAPTER 4

1917
Seeing it Through

On 11 January, Camel's Head School opened as a hospital for wounded troops.

On 19 January, a party of fourteen missionaries arrived safely at Plymouth. They had been held prisoner by the enemy since the early days of the war and were held captive in German East Africa. They were freed by the Belgian forces.

The *Exeter and Plymouth Gazette* of Wednesday 24 January reported the tragic death of an army officer and his wife at the Duke of

Soldiers relax at a military hospital while listening to gramophone records and playing cards.

Cornwall Hotel. They had been found dead on the Monday night by the manager after he tried their door when they failed to come down for dinner. The officer, a captain, aged 40, and his wife, aged 24, had been staying at the hotel since 10 January. They were found dead on their bed with letters beside them and the coroner stated that there was no doubt that this was a case of suicide but that a post-mortem would be performed. The manager stated that the captain was found dressed in full military uniform lying on top of the bed while his wife was under the sheets in full night attire. Glasses were found by the bed with 'chemical substances' within.

The paper went on to report:

> *It is understood that the Captain was under orders for active service. The couple appeared to be devoted to each other and made themselves generally liked. The Captain had seen service during the present war previous to being drafted to a works battalion. The cause of the tragedy will probably be disclosed in letters to be read at the adjourned inquest.*

On 26 January, the officer was named as Captain Hugh Edmund MacDonnell and his wife was named as Helen Aide MacDonnell. Captain MacDonnell was described as a talented man, a distinguished linguist, and an efficient officer. One of the letters found beside the deceased wrote of the 'persistent run if ill luck that had been ours'. He also wrote that his commanding officer would explain 'torments physical and mental that my poor little wife's illness and disappointment of my career have landed me with'.

Medical evidence showed that the captain and his wife had taken cyanide of potassium and a verdict of 'suicide during temporary insanity' was recorded.

On 30 January, the *Western Times* reported that William C. Payne, who was described as 'one of Plymouth's most energetic special constables' had appeared at the Plymouth Police Court the previous day. He was fined £1 for a breach of the Lighting Order on 24 January. PC Damerell stated that he saw an electric light burning at the Norwich Union offices in Westwell Street from 10 pm until 6 am. It was noted that the light wasn't shaded and the blinds were up. Mr Payne explained that he didn't know how the light came to be on and could only think

A service on board HMS Rinaldo *in the Dockyard in 1917. At the beginning of the war,* Rinaldo *was a tender and training ship to HMS* Vivid, *the Royal Naval Reserve at Devonport. During the war, she saw action at West, South and East Africa.*

that a clerk had caught the switch with the sleeve of his coat as he left the office. He stated that he had always done what he could to make sure that the order was adhered to.

On 4 February, the American Consul at Plymouth sent a message to the American Secretary of State in Washington. It read:

> *American steamer,* Housatonic, *loaded with cargo of wheat for the British Government, was torpedoed by German submarine at 12:30 of the 3rd inst. Vessel was warned and total crew of thirty-seven rescued by submarine and towed for ninety minutes toward land. Submarine fired signal to British patrol boat, which subsequently landed the crew at Penzance.*

One of the crew of the *Housatonic*, the second mate, was also on board the American steamer *Gulflight* when she was attacked in the same place on 1 May 1915. The *Gulflight* became the first American victim of U-boat attacks.

The commander of the U-boat that attacked the *Housatonic* told the crew, 'I have orders to sink every vessel coming to England.' The crew had an hour to leave in which time the ship was searched. A quantity of soap was taken, which the commander informed the crew was hard to find in Germany.

The HMNZT *Mokoia* with the 22nd Reinforcements sailed from Wellington on 13 February, arriving at Plymouth. Many would later die at Ypres.

On 19 February, the school at Paradise Road was taken over by the military and the children were housed and taught at St Barnabas's and Belmont Sunday Schools.

On 21 February, newspapers carried the story that 'the port of Plymouth has been closed until further notice to all ships except those of the allies'.

On 1 March, the *Exeter and Plymouth Gazette* carried an advert for H. Samuel of George Street, Plymouth, announcing their one-day sale on watches. Their advert stated: 'Sergeant-Major J J Martin of the 2nd Battalion Scots Regiment writes that he has carried his H Samuel Watch through the South African as well as the present war and it has kept time splendidly.'

On 9 March, the *Exeter and Plymouth Gazette* reported:

> *At a special parade of troops at Devonport, Major-General H P Hickman CB, commanding the Plymouth Garrison, presented awards for bravery. The band of the Devon Regiment, under Mr W Cox, was present.*
>
> *Private J Searle, of the Devon Regiment, received the Distinguished Conduct Medal, which was awarded under the following circumstances:*
>
> > *During an action in which the British trenches were being enfiladed by shell fire by the enemy, Captain Milne called for volunteers to fetch picks and shovels to dig out men who had been buried. Private Searle volunteered for this work and went back across the open ground under very heavy shell fire to the support trenches and brought up picks and shovels. The work then went on of digging out the men who were buried and four machine gunners were rescued out of six.*

On 12 March, the American steamer *Algonquin* was sunk off Plymouth by a German submarine. It was stated that no warning was given and the passengers, of which ten were Americans, barely escaped with their lives. The commander of the U-boat refused to help save the crew or passengers. All passengers made their way to the ship's lifeboats and twenty-seven men were later landed at Plymouth.

The *Algonquin* also carried a cargo of foodstuffs, which was valued at $1, 700,000. The ship belonged to the American Star Line company and had sailed from New York on 20 February.

On 13 March, the *Western Times* reported a story under the headline *A Little Girl's Strategy*. It read:

> *The following story is told by the Secretary of the Ebeneezer Brotherhood, Plymouth, on Sunday afternoon. Taking a pair of boots to a little girl of eleven, whose mother has given way to drink during the father's absence in the North Sea, Mr Elliott was told by a neighbour: 'It's no use, her mother will pawn them for booze.' The child replied: 'No she won't – I'll take care of that.' Calling a few days later, Mr Elliott was pleased to see the girl still wearing the boots and said so. 'You see,' explained the child, 'I've not had 'em off my feet yet!'*

Johnston Terrace, Devonport. The school at Johnston Terrace was taken over to house military personnel from the overcrowded nearby Royal Naval Barracks on 4 April 1917.

On 24 March, the *Yellowstone News* in Montana carried the headline, 'U.S. expected to announce that state of war exists.' The newspaper went on to report that: 'News received from Plymouth that fifteen men, some of them Americans, have been drowned when the American merchantman *Vigilancia* was sunk without warning by a German submarine.' The story also stated that: 'President Wilson is expected, within 48 hours, to indicate definitely that he believes a virtual state of war exists between the United States and Germany.'

On 4 April, the school at Johnston Terrace was taken over to house military personnel from the overcrowded nearby Royal Naval Barracks.

At home life carried on. Entertainment was provided by the theatre and cinema. The *Evening Herald* of 5 April 1917 stated that the Cinedrome in Ebrington Street was showing the latest Pearl White movie while over at the Electric Theatre in Devonport, Olga Petrova

A publicity postcard showing Pearl White. Pearl White was immensely popular during the silent film age and appeared in many popular serials. People continued to flock to cinemas and theatres throughout the war, often for some light entertainment to escape the realities of the conflict.

was appearing in *Playing With Fire*, described as 'a photo-play of exceptional power, giving scope for a wonderful display of histrionic ability by the most beautiful of all Kinema stars'.

On 5 April, the *Evening Herald* reported:

The U.S. Senate has passed the resolution declaring a state of war with Germany by 82 votes to 6 at 11.15pm after 13 hours continuous debate. There was no demonstration when the result was announced.

America joined the war on 6 April 1917.

On 17 April, the *Western Times* reported Reverend Dr Clifford had paid a visit to Plymouth. In his address to the Brotherhood he hailed the revolution in Russia as 'the ringing of the bells of liberty all over Europe and all over the world'. Another momentous event that he said that he was gladdened by and inspired him was the entry into the war of America who he stated were 'led by her most able and competent President'.

He announced: 'The kaiser will have to go!,' which brought much cheering. He continued, 'If they can't receive him at St Helena [laughter] – possibly we can find a place for him somewhere else. The Hohenzollerns must follow the Romanovs and the sovereignty has to become universal'. The last comment brought much cheering.

He went on:

There are monsters at home which we have to destroy. We have got to destroy the drink trade [applause]. We have got to destroy, as far as we can, gambling and lust. We have to work against inhuman conditions, so as to make it possible for men to live a full, free life, crowded with creative endeavour. And we have got to take care that the liberties taken from us are brought back again. The work at home must be done and then you will be prepared to go and do the work for the whole human race.

On 20 April, the Plymouth Education Committee cancelled an order for 20,000 hymn books due to the shortage of paper.

The *Cornishman* of 24 May announced a 'rare treat' for the patrons of the Theatre Royal with the visit of Mr Martin Harvey, 'a well-known tragedian', who was due to perform in his well-received drama, *David Garrick*. The show commenced on 21 May and lasted for the whole week. He was supported by a Miss N. da Silva together with a strong London company.

On 26 May, Samuel Lindsay, aged 36, was seriously injured while working on transport at the Great Western Railway docks after falling from the deck to the quay. He was given medical treatment and taken to the South Devon and East Cornwall Hospital where he died the following day.

On 29 May, the *Western Times* reported on a case of bigamy, which was prosecuted at the Plymouth Police Court. James H. Larmouth, serving at HMS *Defiance*, was accused of marrying Elizabeth Marie Barker while still married to a wife he had been wed to since 1890. Larmouth was arrested in William Street by a Detective-Sergeant Sanders who had a warrant for his arrest. The accused replied that the

The Air Station at Mount Batten. During the final eighteen months of the First World War, RAF Mount Batten operated an important sea-plane base. It was a hive of activity.

case was in the hands of his solicitor who knew the circumstances and that 'his first marriage was a bad one and the second was a good one'. He was remanded until 4 June and released on £20 bail.

During the final eighteen months of the First World War, RAF Mount Batten operated an important sea-plane base. It was a hive of activity and many people watched from the shores of the Hoe as sea-planes roared across Plymouth Sound before taking off.

At the Millbay Recreation Ground and nearby Drill Hall, a Voluntary Aid Detachment Hospital was set up.

A Soldiers' Rest was set up at Mannamead under the guidance of Emmanuel Church.

The American Army opened a YMCA in the Foresters' Hall and also a military hospital at Laira, which was run by a Colonel Dutcher.

During May, three American ships were sunk by U-boats. The crew of one of the ships, the *Dirigo*, were landed safely at Plymouth although one crewman on board, John Ray, was killed. He died while launching one of the lifeboats. All vessels were attacked without warning. The *Dirigo* was attacked by gunfire from the U-boat before being sunk by bombs after being ransacked by the crew of the submarine. The attack took place at 7 am and the survivors were rescued by 9 am. They were cared for by Joseph G. Stephens, the American Consul in Plymouth.

The other two ships attacked were the *Francis M* and the *Barbara*. The *Francis M* was attacked by gunfire on the morning of 18 May. All crew members were rescued and taken to Cadiz.

VAD nurses aid an injured soldier. With the ever-rising amount of casualties arriving back at Britain, there was a great need for assistance at hospitals. Thousands of women answered the call and became part of the Voluntary Aid Detachment (VAD), which aided injured soldiers, sailors and airmen.

The *Barbara* was attacked at 7 am on 24 May and, again, all crew members were saved. They were later landed at Gibraltar.

On 1 June, Captain Urquhart, who was in charge of the *Dirigo*, gave an interview at Plymouth. He said that he had been asleep in the chartroom when the attack took place. He rushed up to the deck to discover the mate giving orders to abandon ship. One lifeboat, containing eleven men, was already in the water while the *Dirigo* was still underway. While trying to reach the boat, Third Mate John Ray fell overboard and drowned. The third shot fired by the submarine hit the *Dirigo* and the U-boat commander ordered the ship to come alongside. An American boat was then used by the German sailors to board the ship. They seized all important papers and documents before blowing it up.

Before they left, the commander of the U-boat shouted to the crew of the *Dirigo*, 'Steer by the wind, the land is not far off.' The crew were later picked up by a fishing boat before being taken back to Plymouth.

The *Dirigo* had set off from New York on 3 May heading towards Havre. Its cargo consisted of mahogany logs and other materials that were valued at $500,000. On board were a crew of thirty-nine men, of which nine were American citizens.

On 25 June, the inquest was held at Plymouth of Flight Sub-Lieutenant Harold Lawrence Crowe, of the Royal Navy Air Service. He was returning from a patrol on 22 June and was about 500 yards from the beach when his aircraft was observed suddenly to nose-dive from 1,500 feet. While falling, it somersaulted and landed in the water

American troops at camp. The Americans entered the war on 6 April 1917. Newspapers in Britain had earlier criticised America for not entering the war. The Western Morning News *had previously written: 'If Americans were in our position they would act precisely as we have done, and might well have improved upon it, at least, in the matter of time. As neutrals they would naturally like to get the best of both worlds, but when the Germans threaten the Americans as well as the British with assassination and pillage on the high seas, the alternative we offer them is at least tempered by mercy and justice.'*

on its back. After locating the crash site the machine and pilot were recovered the following day. The jury stated that death was due to shock caused by a result of injuries accidentally received.

On 26 June, the *Western Times* reported that 800 carters had handed in their notice due to a wages dispute between the Dockers' Union and the Cartowners' Association. The carters received thirty-three shillings a week, including war bonuses, which amounted to ten shillings weekly. On 25 April, through their union, they submitted a demand for an extra seven shillings a week. This was met by an offer of an extra two shillings from the Employers' Association. Without being able to reach an amicable agreement, the carters decided to cease work on 29 June. It was reported that if the men were to leave their jobs, that a dozen large firms, many engaged on government work and many smaller firms would be affected. The stand was being taken because the cost of living was now over 100 per cent above pre-war prices.

On 3 July, it was reported that the son of Reverend Horatio Pack, minister of Courtenay Street Congregational Church, had been awarded the Military Cross. Lieutenant Douglas H. Pack, of the King's Liverpool Regiment, had received the medal for distinguished service in the field.

On 17 July, the *Western Times* reported that a sergeant had been shot on the rifle range at Tregantle. It was alleged that Sergeant Mant had been deliberately shot and killed by Private Thomas Joseph McDonald of the Worcestershire Regiment. McDonald was one of a firing party that had proceeded from Fort Tregantle to the firing range, for musketry practice, early on the previous morning.

The paper reported:

> *As far as can be gathered, McDonald had fired five rounds at one of the ranges and proceeded to another distance for the purpose of firing another five. He took his place on the mound facing the targets with Sergeant Mant lying by his side. It is stated that the latter said to McDonald, 'Come on lad, see what you can do.' It is alleged that McDonald thereupon deliberately turned around and, pointing the rifle at Sergeant Mant, shot him in the left nostril. Lieutenant Wilson and Corporal Owen, seeing what had happened, rushed toward the Private, who is alleged to have pointed the rifle at Owen, who thereupon halted. The*

The army camp at Fort Tregantle. On 17 July 1917, a Sergeant Mant was shot dead by Private Thomas Joseph McDonald of the Worcestershire Regiment while training on the firing range.

> *Lieutenant came on and McDonald, dropping his rifle, was sprung upon by the officer, both he and McDonald rolling down a bank. The Private was promptly secured and taken to Torpoint Police Station where a charge of murder was preferred. Prisoner is stated to have a wife and two children.*

On 28 July, a report from Plymouth announced that the American barque *Carmela* had been sunk by a German submarine. All twenty members of the crew were unharmed and landed safely. The submarine fired four shots at the *Carmela* before the crew took to their boats. They were then ordered to go on board the submarine before being placed under armed guard. The crew of the submarine next looted the ship's stores of coffee and bacon. The Germans were interrupted by a patrol boat, who rescued the crew of *Carmela* before the submarine disappeared for good.

The *Carmela*, weighing 1,379 tons, set sail for the United States on 29 June heading for Havre in France. The crew and their skipper, Captain John A. Johnson, were later sent to Liverpool before returning to New York.

On 6 August, the American Ambassador Dr Walter Hines Page gave an address at the Guildhall in Plymouth. He spoke of 'a method whereby a better mutual understanding of American and British peoples may be achieved'. He went on to say: 'What would the future of the human race be worth if the deliberate barbarism of our enemies overrun the earth? The supreme gift of free government, which this brave island gave to the world, and to which all free lands chiefly owe their freedom, would be swept away. Let the darkness of death overtake us now rather than that the darkness of tyranny should sweep over the whole world of free men.'

His speech went on to emphasise the need of an international companionship between Britain and America.

In August, the 2nd (Home Service) Garrison Battalion, who had been formed in Exeter in June 1916, moved to Plymouth and Falmouth becoming the 5th Battalion of the Royal Defence Corps.

On 12 August, a police constable was called to a house in St Budeaux where he discovered George Robert Melville, aged 17, being attended to by a Dr Thomas. Three fingers on his left hand were almost totally severed. Melville told the constable that he had been walking on the Great Western Railway line near St Budeaux when he was hit by a train. He stated that he did not know if the train had run over his hand or not. Melville was described in news reports as a '1st class boy in the Royal Navy'. He was later taken to the Royal Naval Barracks.

On 5 September, the *Western Times* reported the story of an ex-soldier who had been charged with theft. The story read:

Dressed in civilian clothes and described as a labourer, Henry Foreman, of 3 Cannon Street, Devonport, was charged before Mr P Gayton, in the chair, and Mr P Kelland at the Exeter Police Court yesterday, with stealing between May 10th and 12th from the Higher Barracks, three postal orders, two for £1 and one for 15s.

Prisoner said that he was innocent of the charge. Detective Evans gave evidence to the effect that when arrested at Devonport, the defendant remarked that he knew nothing about the matter. He was told his wife had changed one of the orders at Devonport and he replied 'Yes, I did send that order to her. I had some money about me and I had that order from a chap at the Barracks.' A second postal order, changed by Foreman, had been identified.

The Chief Constable remarked that the defendant had been a sergeant at the Barracks and worked in a department where no letters or postal orders ever came.

He was remanded in custody for a week.

On 10 September, James Richardson was found to have been drunk while in charge of a steamer and was subsequently fined £50 and sentenced to three months imprisonment.

On 19 September, the *Taunton Courier and Western Advertiser* reported on a court-martial at Plymouth. Bugler Percy Bernstock, aged 30, of the Somerset Light Infantry, pleaded not guilty to desertion at Ipswich on 15 June and remaining absent until apprehended by the civil police at Whitechapel on 25 June, dressed in plain clothes. He also pleaded not guilty to losing by neglect his 'regimental necessaries' and equipment. Captain G. R. Leacroft MC of the Somerset Light Infantry produced documents that showed the value of the missing items to be £4 9s. In a written statement, the accused said that he had enlisted with the London Scottish in November 1915 and had to pay a registration fee of £1. At the time of joining, he was informed that he could not be transferred to a different unit.

During training he developed a septic foot and, after being in hospital for three months was recommended for light duties for a lengthy period. He was then examined by the medical board, who classed him as B1 and was then transferred to the Somerset Light Infantry. Another medical board classed him as A and he applied to rejoin his old unit. His name was forwarded to a commanding officer, who said that he regretted that he couldn't be transferred because the Somerset Light Infantry was a regular unit and the London Scottish were Territorials. The accused stated that he felt that he had been treated very badly and that is why he left his unit. He also pointed out that he was Russian and when he had joined the London Scottish, he had lied about his nationality stating that he was English. He, however, said that he felt that he should 'do his share' during the war and had intended joining the Jewish Battalion after the Jewish holidays, but was apprehended before he could do so.

Also appearing at the court-martial was Private Peter Sullivan, aged 19, of the Somerset Light Infantry who pleaded not guilty to disobeying the command of Leading-Sergeant F. J. Davis on 5 September. Sergeant Davis said that he took the accused to the company store-room and ordered him to put on his uniform, which was lying there waiting for him, ready for him to go on parade. The accused refused, with the sergeant repeating the order twice, once in the presence of CSM Howard. CSM T. Howard said that he had ordered the accused to put on the uniform three times but had been disobeyed. Private Sullivan stated that the reason he refused was that he was Irish and had joined the army voluntarily, but had been transferred from the Royal Irish Lancers to the Somerset Light Infantry. He said he would quite happily serve with the Irish Lancers, in which his brother also served, but he would not serve in the Somersets.

Sentences were to be determined at a later date.

On 24 September, troops from the New Zealand Expeditionary Force arrived in Plymouth on route to Salisbury Plain. On leaving Plymouth's Friary Lane Station they were told that food would be laid on for them at their first stop at Exeter Central. However, the train stopped at the Bere Ferrers Station and troops alighted the train from the wrong side straight onto the tracks. They fell straight into the path of the London Waterloo to Plymouth Express and nine men were killed instantly. All were later buried at Efford Cemetery with military honours.

On 12 October, it was reported that Reverend Arthur W. Brown, who had been the Wesleyan Chaplain at Crownhill Barracks in Plymouth, had been severely wounded while serving with the Staffordshire Regiment in France. Several men who were with him were killed by an enemy shell. Reverend Brown suffered contusion of the back and several fractured ribs but was reported to be progressing favourably back home in a hospital in Bristol.

The *Evening Post* carried a story of New Zealanders serving in England. A story from 16 October reported that:

Major H.C. Barclay, R.A.M.C. (Waimate), has been on service at Plymouth and Devonport military hospitals, and was also in charge of Keppel Place Hospital, acting as president of medical boards there. He was then granted leave to make a special study of medical and surgical neurology at the Royal Victoria Hospital at Netley. Major Barclay studied hypnotism in relation to war neurosis and the re-education of men with mental and physical defects, and also studied the use of electrical appliances for the treatment of nerve diseases.

Two escaped German prisoners were recaptured on 22 October on board a neutral ship at Plymouth bound for New York. The men had escaped in France and were discovered hiding in the vessel's coal bunkers.

The Duke of Connaught visited Plymouth on Friday 26 October 1917 and was pleased with the welcome he received. On the Saturday following, his Royal Highness visited the Millbay Voluntary Aid Detachment Hospital as well as the Derriford Convalescent Hospital before lunching with the mayor and mayoress.

On Friday 26 October, the Duke of Connaught visited Plymouth and was pleased with the welcome he received. On Saturday, his Royal Highness visited the Millbay Voluntary Aid Detachment Hospital as well as the Derriford Convalescent Hospital before lunching with the mayor and mayoress. In the afternoon he attended a naval and military parade on Plymouth Hoe and also presented medals. At the parade were 200 bluejackets, 100 each of the Devonshire Regiment and Somerset Light Infantry, fifty each of the Officer Cadet Battalion, Royal Artillery, Royal Engineers and Royal Marines together with twenty Army Service Corps. A total of twenty-eight naval and twenty-five military war medals were presented after the troops had marched by his Royal Highness in fours.

After the parade, the duke met members of the Plymouth Corporation who were the guests of Mrs Astor at tea. Afterwards, he attended a meeting of the Provisional Grand Lodge of Freemasons at the Guildhall and in the evening he was the guest of Major-General and Mrs Hickman at Government House, Devonport.

On Monday 29 October, the musical *The Bing Boys are Here* played at the Theatre Royal and continued for six nights. It was one of the most

George Street and the Theatre Royal. Regular entertainment continued at the Theatre Royal throughout the war with musicals, revues and pantomimes. The Christmas pantomime for 1917, Cinderella, *became one of the theatre's most popular shows and set a box office record at the time.*

popular musicals of the First World War and included the song: *If you were the only girl in the world*. It had previously played at the Alhambra Theatre in London in 1916 when the main star was George Robey.

On 5 November, Frank Tucker, an Army canteen waiter, was fined £25 at a Plymouth court for hoarding 58lb of sugar and 26lb of tea.

On 17 December, the *Western Times* reported on a match between two teams of cadets at Home Park:

> *The Topsham Barracks Cadets took down a team to Home Park on Saturday to oppose the Naval Depot at Devonport and suffered a big reverse, the Depot beating them by 4 goals, 1 dropped goal, 7 tries (45 points) to nil. At half time, the score was 14 points to nil. The cadets were much below full strength. Their best players were Eastwood, Tolmie and Major Ellis.*

On 20 December, Mr Glover of the Theatre Royal, Plymouth, announced that this year's pantomime would be *Cinderella*. The cast was described as 'powerful' and included Plymouth's favourite, Miss Kitty Storrow, who was once more engaged to take the part of the principal boy, Prince Charming. The production boasted no shortage of funny men and the cast included Gus Oxley, who was to play Lord Stonebroke, Cinderella's father. Oxley was no stranger to Plymouth, having appeared on stage there in several well-known companies including *The Bing Boys*. Another 'clever comedian' taking part was Eddie Foy, who played the page.

On 23 December, Petty Officer Alfred S. Baker, who had been a reserve for Plymouth Argyle, died on the *Tornado* when the ship was lost.

An article carried in the *Western Times* of 27 December reported news concerning food ships at Plymouth. It read:

> *Plymouth newspapers have recently been drawing attention to what they describe as the occurrence of ships safely arriving at Plymouth, and then leaving there without unloading, and being torpedoed while on their way to another port. To judge by the frequency with which this and like statements have been repeated, one would think that there must be some strange perversity in the Admiralty or the Ministry of Shipping leading directly to unfortunate incidents. It is contrary to the fact to*

assert that there is frequent repetition of them. They have been rare occurrences, and, previous to a comparatively recent case, there had been nothing of the kind for six months.

The real difficulty at Plymouth is the lack of accommodation at the port, combined with the geographical situation of the place, and the congestion of the railways, both these being conditions profoundly influencing the distribution of perishable supplies.

This will be better understood if it be known that there have been cases of wastage through the putrefaction of meat on its way by rail from Plymouth. The ship recently torpedoed carried 4,000 tons of meat and the port has cold storage for only 400 tons. This is the root of the trouble. The ship in question called at Plymouth on her way to another port and met with disaster as she proceeded there.

The lack of cold storage accommodation at Plymouth will, doubtless, soon be remedied.

Reference had been made to the offer of the Plymouth Corporation of 30 acres of waterside ground for the purpose of creating a great commercial harbour. Whether the project will ever take practical shape, it is impossible to say but, at the present time, when labour is difficult to procure, and when there is so much other and more urgent work to be done, there are no means available for entering upon a gigantic scheme for creating a new commercial port with basins and storehouses at Plymouth.

CHAPTER 5

1918
The Final Blows

In January 1918, sugar was rationed. By the end of April, meat, butter, margarine and cheese were also rationed. Ration cards were issued and people were required to register with their local butcher and grocer. People in Plymouth joined long queues to get basic foods, including potatoes and many other vegetables.

Shopping in wartime. With food rationed, women and children formed long queues, overseen by policemen, to purchase whatever was available. Basic foods like meat and cheese were all in short supply.

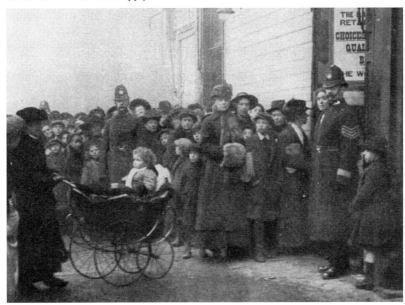

On 8 January, the *Western Times* reported the case of a man who had broken into a cinema in Devonport. The report read:

> *Mr J A Hawke, KC, the Plymouth Recorder, was on Friday, at the Plymouth Quarter Sessions, subjected to an outburst of remarkable insolence. Frederick Baxter, alias Frederick Dobson, aged 32, hawker, pleaded guilty to a charge of having broken into a Devonport Picture Palace and stolen 5s. Asked if he had anything to say before sentence was passed, prisoner made the following statement:*
>
> > *'It's like this here, sir. I don't intend to plead until tears run down my face as large as bananas. I always take the sunshine with the rain and if you intend sending me to prison, I want you to send me for a long term, not because I like it, no far from that, but I have no home, habitation or friends and want somewhere to go until things are better. The next time I have the pleasure of meeting you, which I hope will not be here, I will make you a present of a gold watch as big as a frying pan.'*
>
> *The recorder passed a sentence of 18 months with hard labour.*

On 12 January, the death of Lieutenant R.H. Smith at Herne Bay was recorded as accidental. Smith, the son of a Plymouth journalist, died during an exercise showing recruits how to throw live bombs.

The *Cornishman* of 17 January reported that *Cinderella*, showing at the Theatre Royal in Plymouth, was 'one of the most successful that has been produced in the West Country'. The report said that the show appealed to young and old alike and that thousands of people had already seen it, setting a box office record.

On 22 January, the Plymouth Food Control Committee decided to requisition one-half of the margarine supplies consigned to the Maypole Company. The margarine was to be distributed to retail shops in the most convenient areas to cover the most populous parts of the borough.

During February an appeal for a football appeared in the *Western Times* from members of the Devonshire Regiment serving in France.

A ration book and coupons. Sugar was rationed in January 1918 and by April meat, butter, margarine and cheese were also rationed. Rationing became a way of life and much was in short supply.

A Mr Webber of the Exeter Sports Depot sent one to the mayoress's depot to be forwarded on to the troops. Other donations of footballs were expected and the newspaper commented that 'all would be welcome'. Readers from Plymouth and Exeter were also asked to forward any books and periodicals to the mayoress's depot, which would then be forwarded to the Front.

On 17 February, the Bishop of Exeter paid a visit to the boys' training establishment at Devonport where he confirmed ninety youths and boys on HMS *Powerful* before holding a service on the *Impregnable*.

On 21 February, Viscount Milner, a member of the war cabinet, gave a speech at Plymouth. In his speech, he said:

> *There is but one answer to the German challenge and I will not conceal what that answer involves. Great and wonderful as have been the efforts and endurance of the British nation during the last three and a half years, we must be prepared for greater efforts and hardships in the immediate future, but the more fiercely the storm rages, the higher the spirit of the nation will rise. There are two essential conditions for using our great resources to the full. First, more perfect co-ordination of effort by all the Allies; second, maintenance within the borders of each allied nation of a unity of spirit and purpose, suppression of domestic discord, and the concentration of all efforts on one supreme object – national salvation.*

On 22 February, Lord Milner, a member of the War Cabinet at Plymouth stated:

> *As regards co-ordination of effort among the Allies, more progress has been made in the last three months than in the preceding three years.*

On 19 March, a Lord Roberts Memorial Workshop was opened in Plymouth to provide employment for disabled servicemen.

On 6 April, the *Gloucester Journal* reported:

> *Two soldiers, one a coloured man, died near Plymouth after drinking from a barrel of spirits washed ashore.*

Zeebrugge sailors on board the King George V. *The raid on Zeebrugge on 23 April 1918 by the British Royal Navy effectively put the German naval base at Bruges out of action. The assault was planned and led by Admiral Roger Keyes.*

On 30 April the *Western Times* reported the return of Plymouth troops:

> *Plymouth, on Saturday, accorded an enthusiastic welcome to the men of the Plymouth Division of the Royal Marines when they reached the western port after having taken part in the now famous Naval raid on Zeebrugge and Ostend. The contingent having spent nearly twelve hours in the train of their journey from Deal, right glad were they to alight at Plymouth. They were received by a large crowd, who did not forget to show their appreciation of the brave deeds which had been done in the attack on the Mole. The route from the railway station to the Royal Marines Barracks was lined with enthusiastic sightseers, and as the gallant fellows swung along to the martial strains of the battalion band, the scene was one which will ever live in the memory of those who witnessed it. The whole battalion of the Marines turned out to welcome their brave comrades and Colonel F C Edwards addressed a few words of welcome to the*

Zeebrugge contingent. He congratulated them on their safe return and paid a fitting tribute to every man who had so nobly played his part in the expedition, a thing they would never forget. In after life, they would be able to say, with just pride, 'I was one of the Marines who took part in the fight at Zeebrugge.' They had maintained the best traditions of the Corps; they had taken part in a fight which would never be forgotten as long as the name of Marines exist. They had left behind many a good friend and good comrade; they mourned their loss and deeply sympathised with their relatives, who would remember with pride, when the first bitterness had passed, that their men had died as they would have liked to die, with their face to the foe, and for the honour of the Corps they had served so well.

One of the men who took part in the raid referred in glowing terms to the splendid leadership of the officers. It was, he said, just a hand-to-hand fight but Fritz was not at all keen on the bayonet and, as soon as he could, he got out of the reach of our fellows.

'Our bayonet charges,' he added, 'seemed to put the wind up the enemy.'

Another hero said that they were on the Mole for about an hour and it was one big thrill. Such an hour as this was worth a lifetime. Lieut-Colonel Elliot, DSO, was killed on the Vindictive *just as she was being brought alongside the Mole. The Huns fought very hard and never gave an inch of ground unless forced at the point of their bayonet. They were bayoneted at their guns.*

On 7 May, a boy from Devonport found himself in court after taking an unpaid trip on a train to Exeter. The boy, who was un-named was described as 'a rosy-faced 11 year old Devonport lad'. Chief-Inspector Martin said that the boy was found on the train at St David's Station in Exeter and that he was on his way to see his uncle at Paddington. He gave a false name. When enquiries were made it was found that the boy's father was in the army and the court was told that he had run away several times before. His mother stated that he had taken money and slept out at night. Apart from that, he was said to be of good character and well-behaved at school.

The chairman asked the boy if he would be sorry to be sent to a reformatory to which he replied, 'I don't mind.'

FASHIONS FOR WOMEN IN WAR TIME

THE " SERVICE " UNIFORM
WITH BARBED WIRE TRIMMING AT THE FRONT

A humorous postcard showing fashions for women in war time. This one shows a dress complete with barbed wire on the front. It was drawn by popular cartoonist Reg Carter, who also later drew strips for The Beano *as well as many other comics.*

He added that he wanted to leave home because his sisters told lies about him.

He was fined and was ordered to be sent back to Devonport. His mother was left to pay the fare.

The *North Devon Journal* of 9 May reported the gallantry of a soldier stationed at Woodland, Plymouth. Sergeant A. J. Sanders, of E Company of the Devon regiment was present when a rifle grenade was fired, but due to a defective blank cartridge the grenade failed to fire and fell on the parapet of the firing bay endangering the lives of the occupants of the adjoining bay. Sergeant Sanders quickly picked up the live grenade and threw it clear of the men saving many lives. An entry of the gallant act was recorded on the regimental conduct sheet of Sergeant Sanders as in accordance with the King's Regulations. The incident was recorded as having taken place on 19 April.

On 10 May, the *Western Times* reported the meeting of the Okehampton Branch of the Devon Farmers' Union on Saturday 5 May. The meeting was presided over by Mr A. Knapman, who proposed sending a letter to the Right Honourable George Lambert MP.

The letter, which was read at the meeting, discussed the difficulty of farmers continuing to gather crops while all their men were being called up for the army.

Part of the letter read:

> *We think that the 200 or 300 farmers' men that will be ordered to join up in the western division of Devonshire is not sufficient to justify endangering so many thousands of acres of corn.*
>
> *Instead of further drawing on men engaged in agriculture at such a critical time and before the crops are secured, a great many men could be taken from the Devonport Dockyard where thousands have flocked since the war began, to avoid fighting and to receive a wage out of all proportion to that paid to the boys who are fighting either in the Army or Navy. We are informed their output could be increased if their numbers were decreased and that they were positively in each other's way.*

This brought much applause. The letter continued:

> *We are told that there are quite a number of men in the yard who have a knowledge of agricultural smithing, horse shoeing etc.*
>
> *As so much valuable time is lost by farmers being unable to get their horses shod and implements repaired, we think such men should be placed where so urgently needed in Devon and Cornwall. They could be called back at a few hours' notice should a rush of repairing become necessary as a result of a naval battle.*
>
> *We fear the reason why the Yard is so crowded is to justify the retention of an army of over-lookers and officials and to squander the millions, caring little whether the men earn their money or not.*

On 21 May, a tram strike hit the residents of Plymouth, causing great inconvenience. Only five tramcars remained running while 100 drivers, conductors, cleaners, etc, all went on strike. The service resumed in the afternoon after the Tramways Committee gave a promise that their grievances be aired at a meeting the following day. The dispute arose because some members belonged to the Dockers' Union while others belonged to the Municipal Employers Association, which was not recognised as a trade union. With the object of forcing the men to join the Dockers' Union, notice of a strike was given out late on Friday night and members were told that no tramcars were to run on Saturday morning.

The *Western Times* of 8 June reported:

> *Plymouth Ratepayers' Association have decided to support the notice of a motion by Councillor Pengelly to the effect that no conscientious objector be allowed to remain in the sevice of the Town Council.*

On 21 June, the Devon Women's War Agricultural Committee met at Exeter and a Miss Calmady-Hamlyn reported on the recent recruitment drive at Plymouth, Exeter and Torquay. She said that the response to their appeal had been most satisfactory, better than in other parts of the

The Land Army was set up in Great Britain in 1917. Women played a big role in agricultural work and were asked to sign on for either six months or a year. With many men away fighting, they provided a vital service.

country. She stated at Plymouth that seventy new recruits joined up and that the class of recruits was good, not the 'odds-and-ends found in other towns'. She was pleased that they consisted of daughters of farmers and labourers and were generally country girls. Thousands of girls were still needed and it was suggested that they took their recruitment drive to seaside towns during the summer.

A Miss Nightingale, for the committee stated that since the inauguration of the Land Army movement, 337 women had been accepted with 274 working on farms, forty-seven working for the forage department and sixteen working for the timber cutting section.

On 28 June under the headline *A Draper's Fortune*, the total of John Yeo's estate was announced:

> *Mr John Yeo of Standerton, Plymouth, head of John Yeo and Co. drapers, Plymouth, mayor in 1906 and 1907 and again in 1909 and 1910, who died on May 7th, left a fortune of £102,706, the net personalty being £69,511.*

Submarine chasers SC 47 and SC 258. Chasers were small and fast naval vessels designed to disrupt German submarine warfare. They had been used successfully off the shores of America and arrived in Plymouth in 1918. It was stated that not a single merchant ship was sunk between Lizard Head and Start Point while the sub-chasers were in operation between June and August 1918.

Rear Admiral Sims wrote in his book, *The Victory at Sea*:

Rear Admiral William Sowden Sims. Sims was a commander of the American Naval forces in European waters during the First World War. He went on to write The Victory at Sea *in 1920, which told of his experiences.*

> *By June 30, 1918, two squadrons of American chasers, comprising thirty-six boats, had assembled at Plymouth, England, under the command of Captain Lyman A. Cotten U.S.N. The U.S. destroyer* Parker, *commanded by Commander Wilson Brown, had been assigned to this detachment as a supporting ship. The area, which now formed the new field of operations, was one which was causing great anxiety at that time. It comprehended that sections of the Channel which reached from Start Point to Lizard Head, and included such important shipping ports as Plymouth, Devonport and Falmouth. This was the region in which the convoys, after having been escorted through the submarine zone, were broken up, and from which the individual ships were obliged to find their way to their destinations with greatly diminished protection. It was one of the most important sections in which the Germans, forced to abandon their submarine campaign on the high seas, were now actively concentrating their efforts. Until the arrival of the subchasers, sinkings had been taking place in these waters on a considerable scale. In company with a number of British hunting units, Captain Cotten's detachment kept steadily at work from June 30th until the middle of August, when it became necessary to send it elsewhere. The historical fact is that not a single merchant ship was sunk between Lizard Head and Start Point as long as these subchasers were assisting in the operations.*

The *Western Times* of 2 July reported that Plymouth Co-op had been fined for wasting potatoes. The story read:

Plymouth Co-operative Society were yesterday fined £50 by the Plympton magistrates for permitting potatoes to be wasted at Weir Farm. Evidence for the prosecution was that the police found about 4 tons of potatoes which they considered fit for human food left in heaps for pigs' food. The defendants explained that their potatoes were sorted by a competent woman and only diseased or very small ones were given to the pigs.

On 3 July, it was reported in the *Western Times* that Second-Lieutenant John Crowe, of the Worcester Regiment, who had recently been awarded the Victoria Cross, was a 'Devonport boy'. He was awarded the Victoria Cross for: 'The most conspicuous bravery, determination and skilful leading when the enemy, for the third time having attacked a post in a village, broke past on to the high ground and established a machine-gun and snipers in the broken ground at the back of the village.'

The story continued:

Second-Lieutenant Crowe twice went forward with two NCOs and seven men to engage the enemy, both times in face of active machine-gun fire and sniping. His action was so daring that on each occasion the enemy withdrew from the high ground into the village, where Second-Lieut. Crowe followed them, and himself opened fire on the enemy as they collected in the doorways of the houses.

On the second occasion, taking with him only two men of his party, he attacked two enemy machine-guns which were sweeping the post, killed both the gunners with his rifle and prevented any others from reaching the guns and bringing them in action again.

He then turned upon a party of the enemy who were lined up in front of him, killed several, and the remainder withdrew at once. He captured both the guns, one of which was the Battalion Lewis gun which had been captured by the enemy on the previous day.

Throughout the seven days of operations Second-Lieut. Crowe showed an utter disregard of danger and was recklessly brave.

On 6 July, Sir Robert Kindersley, the chairman of the National War Savings Committee, inaugurated Plymouth's War Weapons Week. He noted that the £25,000,000 a week requested by the Chancellor of the Exchequer the previous October had been reached but he believed that more was needed. He estimated that the war between 1914 and 1918 had cost 'ten thousand millions', and he said that there were only two ways to pay for it either through taxation or savings. He stated:

> *Either we have the grit, character and courage to pay out of savings, or after the war to find ourselves without available capital to enable industry and commerce to enter successfully the contests of the future. Social reconstruction would also make imperative demands on our resources. The old demonstrating habits of extravagance and ostentation must disappear. With saner spending and saving only should we recuperate rapidly from the effects of war.*

On 16 July, it was reported that Major Waldorf Astor, one of the Members of Parliament for Plymouth, had been appointed parliamentary secretary to the minister of food.

On 22 July, Salamanca Day was celebrated by the Devonshire Regiment at Mount Wise in Devonport. Athletic sports took place with substantial prizes offered. There was much competition for the battalion challenge cup, which was won by 'D' company with 'E' company being the runners up. As well as the sporting activities there was also a variety of other entertainment offered.

On 27 July, the *Western Times* reported the court-martial of Devonport Dockyard youths. The article read:

> *A district court-martial was held at the Town Barracks, Exeter, yesterday for the trial of six conscientious objectors. Major R Coleridge was President and Major Wray was the prosecuting officer.*
>
> *Private Thomas Wotton, of the Depot Devon Regiment, was charged with disobeying the command of Captain H G Hawker, to put on uniform at Exeter on Monday, 22nd July. It was stated that accused, who had been stationed at the C O camp at Princetown, objected on conscientious grounds to put on the*

uniform. In a written statement, the accused said he regarded the world as his country, mankind as his brothers, socialism as his religion and regarded the military system as a menace to human life and to human freedom. A previous conviction of 8 months' imprisonment for a similar offence at Hounslow was recorded.

Ernest G Stowell, aged 19, Gloucester Regiment, attached to the Depot Devon Regiment and formerly employed at Devonport Dockyard, pleaded guilty to a similar offence at the Exeter Town Barracks on July 23rd. Accused, in a written statement, quoted the Scriptures to show that military service was opposed to the will of God. He added that he had no animosity against officers of the British Army but hoped that God might have mercy on them and that they might be saved. He admitted that he was, at the time of being called to the Army, employed in Devonport dockyard but that was the result of circumstances over which he had no control. He explained that he had entered the dockyard at the age of 14, as an apprentice to the electrical engineering, and then had no spiritual experience. At the age of 16, he was converted. He was bound to serve in the dockyard by agreement, to break which would have been a criminal offence. Now, however, the Government had violated the terms of his indentures by forcing him into the Army, he was at liberty to act on his convictions. He objected to military service entirely on religious grounds and not in opposition to the Government of the country. It was recorded that Stowell was at Plymouth fined £2 and ordered to be handed over to the military authorities for being an absentee.

Howard Vincent Evans, aged 19, of the Gloucestershire Regiment, attached to the Depot Devon Regiment, pleaded guilty to a similar offence at Exeter on July 23rd. In a written statement, the accused said that the spirit of the army was out of harmony with the word of Christ. He became an apprentice to the electrical engineering in Devonport dockyard in 1912 but then he was without religious convictions and had no scruples in the matter. In the following year, he underwent a change and since 1916, he had been a worker in the spiritual field at Plymouth and had acted as a deputy pastor. It was recorded that he had been fined £2 by the Plymouth magistrates for being an absentee and was handed over to the military.

Trams continued to run throughout the war. On 28 August 1918, a deputation from the Disablement Sub Committee of the Plymouth War Pensions Committee appeared before the Tramways Committee and urged them to appoint discharged disabled servicemen to the role of inspectors, rather than giving the job to women as proposed by the committee.

The other three conscientious objectors mentioned in the article had similar religious convictions.

The Allied counter-offensive began on 8 August 1918. Known also as the Hundred Days Offensive, it marked a period during which the Allies launched a series of attacks on the Central Powers on the Western Front commencing with the Battle of Amiens.

On 28 August, a deputation from the Disablement Sub Committee of the Plymouth War Pensions Committee appeared before the Tramways Committee and urged them to appoint discharged disabled servicemen to the role of inspectors, rather than giving the job to women as proposed by the Tramways Committee. A spokesman for the tramways said that they had always considered discharged disabled men for appointments and had 'given employment to 70 such men'. However, acting under the instructions of the National Service Department, the committee felt that the jobs as inspectors would be best suited to women.

On 7 September, a soldier was caught breaking into a Plymouth bar. Private Patrick Banks, aged 32, appeared before Plymouth magistrates on 9 September charged with 'burglariously breaking and entering the Navy Hotel in Southside Street'. He was accused of stealing cigars and whiskey, etc, valued at fifteen shillings, which was stated as being the property of Mrs Elizabeth Jacobs. Just after midnight, a PC Leat, while on patrol on the Barbican, noticed a back window to the hotel was open and a batten had been removed. This aroused his suspicions and with the help of a postman, he was able to waken the inmates of the house at the front while the policeman waited at the back. When the bar was searched, Banks was found in the front bar. He declined to give any reason for his presence there and stated, 'You can put down what you like – it makes no difference to me.'

He was remanded for a week while police made further enquiries.

On 9 September, three stowaways appeared before the Plymouth Bench. Harry Jackson, aged 16, Maurice Frederick Brenner, aged 17, and James Nicholls, aged 16, all from London, were found on a steamer arriving at Plymouth. They told a Detective Sergeant Cloke that they secreted themselves on the vessel before it left Tilbury. Brenner told the magistrates that it was his aim to get to America and join the army or navy there.

A topical postcard featuring a Tommy at the Front showing a soldier protecting his rear end with the caption 'I ain't riskin' havin' me bloomin' brains blown out'. Even with all that went on around them, British Tommies still kept their sense of humour.

Mr Frank Phillips, who represented the owners of the steamer, said that the practice of men secreting themselves on steamers travelling to America was becoming more common.

The Bench sent the three stowaways to prison for a week while endeavours were made for them to be 'assisted by some organisation'.

On 10 September, the Board of Agriculture confirmed that a dog in Plymouth had been discovered to have rabies and there were several other cases under suspicion. A number of people had been bitten by suspected dogs. By November, there were seventy-two cases in Devon and Cornwall. Dogs were barred from leaving the counties and movement of dogs outside Devon and Cornwall was prohibited.

The *Western Times* of 11 September contained the names and details of two Plymouth soldiers who had been awarded the DCM. The article read:

8640 Pte. A/L/Cpl. AC Johns, Devon R. (Devonport).
For conspicuous gallantry and devotion to duty when commanding a section in a counter-attack, which was hastily organised from the men at HQ details. He led the section with the greatest courage in the face of heavy fire at point-blank range, until, with only two men left, he reached and captured a gun, killing the team. On his own initiative, he advanced further until he came upon a party of fifty of the enemy, whom he forced to surrender. After this, being unable to advance, he occupied with the remaining two of his men, a position, and held it till nightfall. His courage and devotion to duty were most marked.

37606 Pte. J Killeen, Gloucester R. (Plymouth).
For conspicuous gallantry and devotion to duty. He went through our artillery barrage by himself and single-handed killed two of the enemy who were holding up the flank of his company with a machine-gun. He led parties forward to cut off the enemy and brought in a considerable number of prisoners. He showed a splendid example of initiative, personal courage and devotion to duty.

The *Aberdeen Journal* of 13 September reported more about the outbreak of rabies in Plymouth. The Department of Agriculture and

Technical Instruction for Ireland issued a four-month banning order preventing the transport of dogs from Great Britain to the Irish mainland.

On 21 September, Dr W. H. Page, the American Ambassador, was presented with the honorary freedom of the Borough of Plymouth, enclosed in a silver model of the Mayflower.

On 3 October, the *Liverpool Echo* reported:

> *During a court martial at Plymouth, a soldier of the British West India Regiment objected to be sworn on the New Testament. He said that he was a Materialist, and would swear by a fruit or a vegetable, any of the works of Nature or anything mechanical. Asked if a watch would do, he said it would, and he was sworn while holding the president's watch in his hand.*

Stokers on board a ship. Stokers played a vital part in the running of a naval ship. They not only stoked coal into the boilers of older ships but also undertook diving and engineering work. All were trained for fieldcraft and were taught how to use firearms as part of their basic training.

The *Western Times* of 8 October carried the story of George Herbert Burr who had appeared before Plymouth magistrates on 7 October and pleaded guilty to a charge of desertion. Burr, a stoker in the RN was found to have a certificate of discharge upon him when he was arrested but it was shown that this was bought from a relative for £10.

Burr was handed over to an escort to be taken to London to give evidence against the relative.

On 28 October, the funeral of Agnes Weston was reported in the *Western Times*:

> *At the funeral of Miss Agnes Weston of Devonport, the coffin was carried on a gun-carriage drawn by bluejackets, the bearers being petty officers of the Navy.*

In November, Admiral Bristol, who was a member of the United States Navy, said at an American boxing match at Plymouth, that 'it was the boxing spirit which prompted Britain to turn upon our enemy as though it were the first round of a fight'.

In Europe, the Hundred Days Offensive effectively pushed the Germans out of France, forcing them beyond the Hindenburg Line, which ultimately led to an armistice.

The *Evening Herald* of 11 November 1918 carried joyous news:

> *News of the signing of the armistice reached us this morning before 9 o'clock through the courtesy of the Admiralty Headquarters at Mount Wise. A veritable pandemonium arose in the Dockyard and district: scores of sirens rent the air with their shrill blasts and big steamer horns boomed out their deep-throated message. At last the world war had come to an end. School children demonstrated to their hearts' content, marching along the principal streets, singing and cheering and exchanging greetings on all sides. One procession had as leader the ubiquitous Charlie Chaplin replete with moustache, cane and preposterous boots.*

On Tuesday 12 November 1918, the *Western Morning News* carried the headline, 'CRUSHING ARMISTICE TERMS'. The article stated:

The crowd at Buckingham Palace on Armistice Day. Thousands of cheering spectators lined the streets to celebrate the end of the war.

Armistice celebrations in George Street, Plymouth, in November 1918. Thousands of people turned out on the streets, smiling, cheering and waving flags. News of the armistice was first received in Plymouth by wireless from the Admiralty. Ships blew their sirens and flags were quickly run up as processions of people formed in the street.

The last shot, it is to be presumed and hoped, has been fired in the greatest war ever known.

At 5 o'clock yesterday morning the armistice was signed by the plenipotentiaries and came into operation six hours later (11 a.m.).

As the end of the war was announced, people came out onto the streets in their thousands to celebrate. Union Street was full of cheering, smiling crowds as was the rest of the main part of the town. The offices of the Evening Herald in Russell Street regularly posted notices in their window of the latest updates.

The war had been a long and bloody one. Plymouth had played a major part in the struggle supplying ships, weapons and troops. Men from all around the world had passed through the port on their way to the conflict. With the war over, there wasn't a family in Plymouth who hadn't lost a son, father, nephew, uncle or brother. There were tremendous celebrations in the streets as the end of the war was announced but the effects of the war lasted for years to come.

Armistice celebrations with many happy faces and much flag-waving. American flags were waved alongside British ones and everyone was jubilant that the war was finally over.

Bibliography

Books

A History of Plymouth and her Neighbours C.W. Bracken (SR Publishers, 1931)

Aspects of Saltash Bruce E. Hunt (BEH Publication, 2009)

100 Years of the Evening Herald James Mildren (Bossiney Books, 1994)

125 Years with The Western Morning News James Mildren (Bossiney Books, 1985)

Plymouth Pictures from the Past Guy Fleming (Devon Books, 1995)

Plymouth, A New History Crispin Gill (Devon Books, 1993)

The Victory at Sea Rear Admiral William Sowden Sims and Burton J. Hendrick (John Murray, 1920)

The Story of Plymouth R.A.J. Walling (Westaway, 1950)

Devon in the Great War, 1914-1918 Gerald Wasley (Devon Books, 2000)

Websites

BBC History www.bbc.co.uk/history

Cyberheritage www.cyber-heritage.co.uk

The Great War 1914 – 1918 http://www.greatwar.co.uk/

Greens On Screen www.greensonscreen.co.uk

The Mighty Mighty Whites http://www.mightyleeds.co.uk/

Brian Moseley's Plymouth Data site www.plymouthdata.info

World War One Battlefields www.ww1battlefields.co.uk

Newspapers

The Aberdeen Journal, The Cornishman, The Coventry Evening Telegraph, The Dundee Courier, The Eugene Register, The Exeter and Plymouth Gazette, The Evening Herald, The Evening Telegraph, The

Evening Post, The Fielding Star, The Gloucester Journal, The Graphic Newspaper, The Hull Daily Mail, The Illustrated London News, The Illustrated War News, The Journal of Commerce, The Liverpool Echo, The London Gazette, The Manchester Evening News, The Newburgh Journal, The New York Times, The North Devon Journal, The Quebec Telegraph, The Poverty Bay Herald, The Saskatoon Star of Phoenix, The Sydney Mail, The Taunton Courier and Western Advertiser, The Times, The Weekly Miami Metropolis, The Western Daily Mercury, The Western Daily Press, The Western Morning News, The Western Times, The Yellowstone News of Montana, The Yorkshire Post.

Index